Mastering Advance Data Analytics

Machine Learning, Data Mining and Analytic Thinking

Dr. Alex Harper

Table of Contents

Chapter 1: Introduction to Advanced Data Analytics and Analytic Thinking

Overview of Advanced Data Analytics and Its Role in Modern Business and Technology

In today's data-driven world, advanced data analytics stands at the intersection of innovation, strategic decision-making, and operational efficiency. Unlike basic analytics, which focuses on descriptive insights and surface-level trends, advanced data analytics delves into predictive and prescriptive analytics, uncovering the deeper insights and foresight needed for businesses to thrive in a competitive landscape. Through methods such as machine learning, data mining, and analytic thinking, advanced data analytics transforms raw data into actionable insights, driving value across every sector from finance and healthcare to retail and entertainment.

1. The Evolution of Data Analytics: From Descriptive to Advanced

Historically, data analytics began as a tool for reporting on past events. Descriptive analytics provided an understanding of what happened, and diagnostic analytics answered why it happened. However, as organizations amassed vast amounts of data and computational power increased, there emerged a need for predictive and prescriptive analytics, which allow businesses to anticipate future trends and optimize decision-making processes. Advanced data analytics leverages complex statistical methods, algorithms, and computational power to go beyond traditional analysis, enabling proactive decision-making that is essential for navigating today's fast-paced business world.

2. Why Advanced Data Analytics Matters in Modern Business

Advanced data analytics is essential in modern business for several reasons. First, it enables a competitive edge. Companies that effectively use data to drive insights can develop more accurate market strategies, create tailored customer experiences, and optimize operational efficiency, setting them apart from competitors. In addition, advanced data analytics empowers companies to better understand consumer behavior, predict demand fluctuations, and innovate new products and services that cater to evolving customer needs.

Consider industries like finance, where predictive models assess credit risk, or healthcare, where machine learning algorithms predict patient outcomes. These applications save time, reduce costs, and improve service quality, exemplifying the crucial role of advanced data analytics in both business success and customer satisfaction.

3. The Components of Advanced Data Analytics

Advanced data analytics consists of several interconnected components that collectively generate deep, actionable insights. These components include:

- **Machine Learning (ML)**: ML algorithms learn from historical data to make predictions or decisions without explicit programming. From supervised and unsupervised learning to reinforcement learning, machine learning enables complex pattern recognition and automation in tasks like recommendation engines and predictive maintenance.

- **Data Mining**: Data mining identifies hidden patterns, correlations, and anomalies in large datasets, often leading to insights that inform strategic business decisions. Techniques like clustering, association rule mining, and anomaly detection are fundamental to uncovering valuable insights from data.
- **Analytic Thinking**: Analytic thinking involves a systematic approach to solving problems through data-driven decision-making. It requires breaking down complex challenges, hypothesizing potential solutions, testing with data, and refining insights. Analytic thinking forms the basis for a structured, hypothesis-driven approach to complex data analysis.

4. The Impact of Advanced Data Analytics on Technology and Innovation

With the rise of big data and advancements in computational power, advanced data analytics has fueled innovations in fields like artificial intelligence, automation, and IoT (Internet of Things). Data-driven technologies are reshaping industries, automating mundane tasks, and enhancing human capabilities. In the retail sector, for instance, data analytics personalizes the customer journey through targeted advertising and recommendation systems. Meanwhile, in manufacturing, predictive maintenance uses analytics to foresee equipment failures, preventing costly downtime.

Furthermore, advanced analytics plays a key role in the development of smart cities, autonomous vehicles, and medical diagnostics, marking an era where data-powered insights continuously push the boundaries of what technology can achieve.

5. Setting the Stage for a Data-Driven Culture

To harness the full potential of advanced data analytics, businesses must cultivate a data-driven culture. This entails aligning organizational goals with data-driven strategies, investing in talent and technology, and promoting analytic thinking at every level. Leaders play a pivotal role in fostering this culture by advocating for data-backed decision-making, encouraging continuous learning, and enabling cross-functional collaboration.

A data-driven culture not only enhances productivity but also fosters innovation, empowering employees to leverage data insights in creative, impactful ways. When every team member—from the C-suite to frontline employees—understands the value of data and analytics, businesses become more resilient and agile in adapting to change.

Conclusion

Advanced data analytics is transforming the way organizations operate, innovate, and compete. In an era where data is abundant and customer expectations are high, businesses that fail to leverage advanced analytics risk falling behind. By embracing machine learning, data mining, and analytic thinking, companies can navigate complexities, anticipate changes, and make informed decisions that drive lasting success. This chapter has introduced the foundational principles and significance of advanced data analytics, setting the stage for a deeper exploration of the techniques and methodologies that will define the future of data-driven decision-making.

Introduction to Machine Learning, Data Mining, and Analytic Thinking as Critical Skills for Data-Driven Decisions

In the modern landscape of business and technology, data is often referred to as "the new oil." However, data on its own is merely a raw resource; its true value is unlocked through the skills and techniques that transform it into actionable insights. Among these, machine learning, data mining, and analytic thinking stand out as foundational competencies that drive impactful, data-driven decisions. Each of these skills contributes uniquely to the analytics process, creating a robust framework that allows organizations to extract maximum value from their data.

1. Machine Learning: The Backbone of Predictive Analytics
Machine learning (ML) is a branch of artificial intelligence that enables computers to learn from and make predictions based on data without explicit programming for each task. Unlike traditional programming, where rules and logic are predefined, ML algorithms identify patterns and relationships within datasets and use these insights to make informed predictions or decisions. This capability makes machine learning a

powerful tool for organizations that want to harness historical data to predict future trends and outcomes.

Machine learning's applications span a variety of industries. In finance, for instance, ML models assess credit risks and detect fraudulent transactions. In healthcare, they predict patient outcomes and optimize treatment plans. In retail, they personalize product recommendations and forecast demand. As a critical skill, machine learning empowers data analysts and decision-makers to move beyond descriptive statistics to predictive analytics, where they can anticipate what is likely to happen and make proactive adjustments.

Key components of machine learning that are vital for data-driven decisions include:

- **Supervised Learning**: Algorithms learn from labeled data, making it ideal for classification and regression tasks, such as predicting sales or categorizing customer feedback.
- **Unsupervised Learning**: Algorithms work with unlabeled data to uncover hidden patterns, such as customer segmentation through clustering.
- **Reinforcement Learning**: The algorithm learns by interacting with an environment, making it suitable for dynamic applications like robotics and game theory.

2. Data Mining: Uncovering Hidden Patterns and Relationships

Data mining is the process of exploring large datasets to identify hidden patterns, correlations, and anomalies. It provides a powerful way to transform raw data into valuable insights, allowing businesses to understand not just what happened but also why it happened. This deeper understanding supports the development of informed, strategic decisions.

The process of data mining involves several techniques:

- **Clustering**: Grouping data points with similar characteristics, often used for customer segmentation and market analysis.
- **Association**: Finding relationships between variables, frequently applied in market basket analysis to determine product co-purchase patterns.
- **Anomaly Detection**: Identifying unusual patterns or outliers, which is useful for fraud detection, network security, and quality control.

By mastering data mining techniques, analysts can unlock insights that may not be immediately apparent. For example, a retailer could analyze purchase patterns to understand which products are often bought together, enabling targeted promotions and increasing revenue. In healthcare, data mining helps identify patterns in patient records, which can lead to better diagnostic methods and treatment protocols.

Data mining equips organizations with the ability to delve deeper into their data, making it an essential skill for anyone involved in advanced analytics.

3. Analytic Thinking: The Foundation of Insightful Decision-Making

While machine learning and data mining provide powerful technical tools, analytic thinking is the mindset that makes these tools effective. Analytic thinking involves a systematic, logical approach to problem-solving. It's about breaking down complex issues, hypothesizing solutions, testing with data, and refining conclusions based on evidence.

Analytic thinking goes beyond technical proficiency; it requires a curiosity-driven approach to understanding data and the stories it can tell. It enables data analysts to:

- **Ask the Right Questions**: Effective analytics begins with asking questions that data can answer. Analytic thinking helps frame questions that are specific, measurable, and aligned with business goals.
- **Identify Key Metrics**: By focusing on relevant metrics, analysts can avoid the trap of analysis paralysis and concentrate on data that drives actionable insights.
- **Connect Data to Business Goals**: Analytic thinking ensures that every data-driven decision is anchored in strategic business objectives, enhancing the impact of analytics on organizational success.

In practical terms, analytic thinking allows analysts to tackle problems creatively and adaptively. For example, if a company experiences a drop in customer satisfaction, an analytically minded data analyst might examine not only direct survey feedback but also indirect indicators, such as customer churn rates, purchase history, and social media sentiment. By connecting diverse data sources and developing a nuanced view of the problem, analytic thinking can reveal insights that might otherwise go unnoticed.

4. The Synergy of Machine Learning, Data Mining, and Analytic Thinking

Together, machine learning, data mining, and analytic thinking create a powerful framework for making data-driven decisions. Machine learning provides the predictive power, data mining uncovers hidden patterns, and analytic thinking ensures that insights are actionable and aligned with business objectives. When combined, these skills enable organizations to go beyond retrospective analysis and static reports, creating a proactive, responsive approach to analytics.

For instance, consider a telecommunications company aiming to reduce customer churn. Machine learning algorithms could predict which customers are likely to leave, data mining could reveal patterns and reasons behind customer dissatisfaction, and analytic thinking would guide the interpretation of these findings into strategic actions, such as personalized retention campaigns or product improvements.

Conclusion

Machine learning, data mining, and analytic thinking are indispensable skills for anyone looking to leverage advanced data analytics effectively. As critical components of the analytics toolbox, these skills empower professionals to uncover insights, predict trends, and make well-informed, data-driven decisions. Mastering these techniques is essential for individuals and organizations aiming to remain competitive in an increasingly data-centric world. In the following chapters, we will delve deeper into each of these areas, exploring practical applications, best practices, and real-world examples that demonstrate their transformative potential.

Differentiation from Basic Analytics and Setting the Foundation for Advanced Concepts

The journey from basic to advanced data analytics is a transformative leap that expands the scope and depth of insights that organizations can derive from their data. While basic analytics focuses on understanding past events and answering "what happened," advanced data analytics goes further, diving into "why it happened," "what is likely to happen next," and "what actions should be taken." This progression from descriptive to predictive and prescriptive insights provides organizations with the foresight and actionable recommendations necessary to stay competitive in an increasingly data-driven world.

1. Basic Analytics: The Foundation of Data Understanding

Basic analytics, also known as descriptive analytics, serves as the entry point for data analysis. It involves collecting, organizing, and summarizing historical data to gain a high-level understanding of trends and patterns. Techniques such as basic statistics, charts, and reports allow organizations to monitor key performance indicators (KPIs), track past performance, and identify areas of concern or opportunity.

However, while basic analytics provides valuable hindsight, it has limitations:

- **Limited to Past Insights**: Basic analytics can only describe past events, offering little in the way of predictive power.
- **Lacks Depth**: By focusing on surface-level data, basic analytics may overlook the underlying causes of observed trends.
- **Static Insights**: Descriptive analytics doesn't adapt to new data in real-time, making it less dynamic for fast-paced decision-making.

For example, a retail store might use basic analytics to identify that sales increased by 15% in the last quarter. However, without understanding why this increase occurred, or whether it will continue, the insight remains limited in scope and impact.

2. Advanced Data Analytics: Moving from Insight to Action

Advanced data analytics builds upon the foundation of basic analytics by incorporating more sophisticated techniques, such as predictive modeling, machine learning, and prescriptive analytics. By leveraging these advanced methods, organizations can gain deeper insights, anticipate future trends, and make data-driven decisions that proactively shape outcomes. Advanced data analytics not only reveals "what" happened but also explains "why" it happened and "what might happen next."

Key differentiators of advanced data analytics include:

- **Predictive Power**: Advanced analytics uses statistical models and machine learning algorithms to forecast future outcomes, helping organizations anticipate trends and make informed decisions.

- **Root Cause Analysis**: Through techniques like data mining, advanced analytics uncovers the root causes of patterns, allowing companies to understand and address the factors influencing performance.
- **Actionable Insights**: Prescriptive analytics takes things a step further, offering recommendations for action, which is invaluable for strategic planning and operational optimization.

In our retail example, advanced analytics might use predictive models to forecast sales for the next quarter, taking into account seasonal trends, marketing campaigns, and customer behavior patterns. This foresight allows the store to plan its inventory, marketing, and staffing accordingly.

3. The Stages of Advanced Analytics: From Descriptive to Prescriptive

To understand the spectrum of data analytics, it's helpful to break it down into four progressive stages:

- **Descriptive Analytics**: The most basic level, focused on summarizing past data to identify what happened. It answers questions like, "What were our total sales last year?" or "How many customers did we acquire?"
- **Diagnostic Analytics**: Building upon descriptive analytics, diagnostic analytics aims to understand why events occurred. For instance, it might analyze why sales in a particular region declined by examining customer demographics, market conditions, or competitor actions.

- **Predictive Analytics**: This stage leverages statistical models and machine learning to forecast future outcomes. Predictive analytics answers questions like, "What will sales look like next quarter?" or "Which customers are most likely to churn?"
- **Prescriptive Analytics**: The most advanced stage, prescriptive analytics, provides actionable recommendations based on predictive insights. It answers questions such as, "What marketing strategies should we implement to increase customer retention?" or "How can we optimize our supply chain to reduce costs?"

By progressing through these stages, organizations move from simple reporting to dynamic, proactive decision-making, unlocking greater strategic value from their data.

4. Setting the Foundation for Advanced Concepts

Understanding the differentiation between basic and advanced analytics is the first step toward embracing the methodologies that drive advanced analytics. A strong foundation in basic analytics provides the necessary skills in data handling, visualization, and statistical analysis. However, to transition to advanced analytics, it is essential to build expertise in areas like machine learning, data mining, and statistical modeling.

Core areas to focus on when advancing in data analytics include:

- **Statistical Analysis and Machine Learning**: Mastering these techniques allows data analysts to build models that not only describe but also predict and optimize.

- **Data Mining and Pattern Recognition**: Identifying patterns, correlations, and anomalies within large datasets is critical for uncovering valuable insights.
- **Analytic Thinking and Strategy**: Beyond technical skills, analytic thinking enables professionals to align data initiatives with organizational goals, ensuring that insights are not only accurate but also relevant and actionable.

This shift toward advanced analytics represents a strategic evolution for organizations. While basic analytics allows companies to understand past events, advanced analytics empowers them to shape the future by making informed, proactive decisions based on data-driven insights.

Conclusion

The difference between basic and advanced analytics is profound, not just in the complexity of techniques but in the impact it can have on decision-making. As businesses navigate an increasingly competitive and data-saturated landscape, advanced data analytics provides the tools and frameworks necessary to stay ahead. This chapter has highlighted the importance of moving beyond descriptive insights and setting the foundation for advanced analytic techniques that will be explored in greater detail in subsequent chapters. By understanding this evolution, readers are now prepared to dive into the world of advanced analytics, unlocking the skills and strategies that lead to smarter, data-driven decisions.

Chapter 2: Data-Driven Mindset: From Analytic Thinking to Strategy

Developing an Analytic Mindset for Real-World Problem-Solving

In a data-rich environment, having the right tools and technologies is only part of the equation for effective problem-solving. The ability to apply data to real-world challenges requires an analytic mindset—a way of thinking that emphasizes curiosity, critical evaluation, and a strategic approach to finding solutions. An analytic mindset combines technical skills with a problem-solving framework, guiding decisions that are grounded in data but responsive to the complexities of real-world scenarios. This chapter explores the elements of an analytic mindset and how it can be developed to tackle both immediate and strategic challenges.

1. What is an Analytic Mindset?

An analytic mindset is an approach to thinking that prioritizes evidence, curiosity, and a structured approach to problem-solving. Unlike traditional decision-making, which may rely on intuition or personal experience, an analytic mindset seeks to ground each decision in data and objective reasoning. This mindset is vital in today's competitive landscape, where access to quality data can turn insight into a powerful advantage.

Characteristics of an analytic mindset include:

- **Curiosity**: A desire to understand the "why" behind every event or observation, leading to deeper insights and comprehensive analysis.

- **Structured Thinking**: The ability to break down complex problems into manageable components, ensuring that each aspect of the issue is examined and understood.
- **Objectivity**: An emphasis on data and empirical evidence, reducing personal biases that may distort conclusions.
- **Strategic Focus**: Aligning analysis with broader organizational goals, ensuring that data-driven decisions support long-term strategy.

2. The Role of Analytic Thinking in Problem-Solving

Analytic thinking is the foundation of a data-driven mindset. It enables professionals to look beyond surface-level information and dive into the root causes of problems. By approaching challenges analytically, one can avoid knee-jerk reactions and instead develop a thoughtful, strategic response. Analytic thinking is particularly valuable in complex or high-stakes situations where data is abundant but not immediately clear.

The problem-solving process within an analytic mindset includes several key steps:

- **Defining the Problem**: An analytic mindset begins by clearly defining the problem to be solved, identifying specific questions that data can help answer.
- **Data Gathering and Assessment**: Collecting and critically evaluating data ensures that analysis is based on reliable, relevant information.
- **Hypothesis Formation**: Developing potential explanations or hypotheses guides the focus of the

analysis, ensuring that the approach is logical and systematic.

- **Testing and Analysis**: Using data to test hypotheses, either confirming or refuting initial assumptions.
- **Interpretation and Application**: Translating findings into actionable insights that address the original problem, contributing to real-world decision-making.

For example, imagine a company experiencing a sudden drop in customer satisfaction scores. An analytic approach would involve defining potential causes (e.g., product quality, service issues, or external factors), gathering relevant data (e.g., customer feedback, service records), forming hypotheses, and analyzing results to identify specific actions to improve satisfaction.

3. Curiosity as the Catalyst for Insight

Curiosity drives the analytic mindset, pushing professionals to ask questions and dig deeper into data. A curious analyst doesn't just accept trends or findings at face value; they seek to understand the underlying causes, patterns, and anomalies. Curiosity fuels exploration and discovery, often leading to insights that may not be immediately obvious.

Encouraging curiosity in a data-driven environment involves:

- **Questioning Assumptions**: Curiosity helps analysts avoid confirmation bias by challenging pre-existing assumptions and exploring alternative explanations.
- **Exploring "What If" Scenarios**: Curious analysts often conduct exploratory analyses to test different scenarios, such as how changing one factor affects the outcome.

- **Identifying Outliers**: Instead of dismissing outliers, curious analysts examine these data points to understand why they deviate, often revealing critical insights about unusual behaviors or market segments.

Curiosity is essential in problem-solving because it broadens the scope of analysis, leading to a more comprehensive understanding of the situation at hand.

4. Structured Thinking: The Framework for Solving Complex Problems

Structured thinking is the ability to break down complex problems into logical steps, making the analysis process more manageable and efficient. When faced with a complex challenge, structured thinking helps analysts approach the problem systematically, examining each component before moving on to the next.

A structured approach to problem-solving involves:

- **Decomposing the Problem**: Breaking down the main problem into smaller, more specific issues or questions.
- **Prioritizing Elements**: Identifying which aspects of the problem are most critical, focusing resources on areas with the greatest impact.
- **Step-by-Step Analysis**: Tackling each component systematically, ensuring that insights are built on a solid foundation.

Structured thinking is particularly valuable in high-stakes or time-sensitive situations, where clear, logical reasoning is essential. By following a structured framework, analysts can ensure that each stage of the analysis is methodical, leading to thorough and accurate conclusions.

5. Objectivity and Bias Reduction in Analysis

One of the greatest challenges in data-driven decision-making is ensuring objectivity. Personal biases, preconceived notions, and organizational pressures can all influence how data is interpreted. An analytic mindset includes a commitment to objectivity, striving to let the data speak for itself without undue influence from subjective factors.

Ways to maintain objectivity include:

- **Data Validation**: Cross-referencing data sources and verifying accuracy to avoid errors that could mislead the analysis.
- **Avoiding Confirmation Bias**: Actively seeking evidence that contradicts initial hypotheses to ensure a balanced perspective.
- **Peer Review**: Sharing findings with colleagues for feedback, allowing others to challenge assumptions and provide alternative viewpoints.

By maintaining objectivity, analysts can make decisions based on factual evidence, reducing the risk of biased conclusions that could lead to poor strategic choices.

6. Aligning Analytics with Strategic Goals

An analytic mindset is not only about solving isolated problems but also about contributing to broader organizational objectives. Aligning analytics with strategy ensures that every data-driven insight supports the company's mission, vision, and goals.

To achieve strategic alignment, analysts should:

- **Understand the Business Context**: Familiarize themselves with organizational goals, industry trends, and competitive pressures.
- **Focus on High-Impact Analysis**: Prioritize analytics projects that have a clear, measurable impact on strategic objectives.
- **Communicate Insights Effectively**: Present findings in a way that resonates with decision-makers, translating data into actionable recommendations that drive value.

Strategic alignment adds context and direction to data analysis, ensuring that insights are relevant and actionable at an organizational level.

Conclusion

Developing an analytic mindset for real-world problem-solving goes beyond mastering technical skills; it requires a mindset rooted in curiosity, structured thinking, objectivity, and strategic alignment. By cultivating these qualities, data professionals can tackle complex challenges with confidence, transforming data into meaningful insights that drive effective decision-making. This chapter has outlined the elements of an analytic mindset, setting the stage for advanced strategies and techniques that will be explored in the following chapters. With this foundation, readers are better equipped to approach data-driven problem-solving with purpose and precision.

Connecting Data Analytics to Strategic Goals and Long-Term Business Objectives

In a data-driven organization, analytics is more than a set of tools or techniques; it is a critical function that aligns with and supports the company's strategic goals and long-term objectives. Connecting analytics to broader business goals involves embedding data-driven thinking into every level of decision-making, ensuring that every insight contributes to the company's mission, vision, and competitive advantage. This chapter examines how to integrate data analytics with strategic goals, from identifying impactful metrics to fostering collaboration and creating a culture of data-driven decision-making.

1. The Role of Data Analytics in Shaping Business Strategy

In today's competitive landscape, strategic decisions cannot rely on intuition alone. Data analytics offers a way to make informed, evidence-based decisions that align with the company's long-term vision. By connecting analytics to strategy, organizations can:

- **Anticipate Market Trends**: Using data to analyze customer behavior, industry shifts, and economic conditions helps businesses stay ahead of market trends.
- **Identify Growth Opportunities**: Analytics reveals new revenue streams, customer segments, or market niches that may be untapped.

- **Optimize Operations**: Data-driven insights improve efficiency and productivity, driving cost savings and process improvements.
- **Enhance Customer Satisfaction**: Analytics can deepen understanding of customer needs and preferences, enabling tailored offerings and improved customer experiences.

When data analytics aligns with strategy, it enables organizations to operate more proactively, adapting quickly to changes and seizing new opportunities.

2. Identifying and Prioritizing Key Performance Indicators (KPIs)

A critical step in connecting analytics to strategic goals is selecting key performance indicators (KPIs) that reflect the organization's objectives. KPIs are quantifiable metrics that track progress toward specific goals, helping companies measure success and make adjustments as needed. The right KPIs enable organizations to monitor performance, make data-driven adjustments, and achieve strategic outcomes.

When selecting KPIs, consider the following:
- **Alignment with Strategic Goals**: KPIs should directly relate to the organization's objectives, such as increasing market share, improving customer retention, or enhancing operational efficiency.
- **Actionability**: KPIs should be actionable, meaning that tracking them leads to insights that inform decision-making and potential changes.

- **Relevance to Stakeholders**: Different departments and stakeholders may have unique KPIs, but all should contribute to overarching business goals.

For example, a company focused on customer satisfaction might track KPIs like Net Promoter Score (NPS), customer retention rates, and average response time. In contrast, a company prioritizing growth might focus on KPIs like market share, customer acquisition cost, and revenue growth.

3. Embedding Analytics in Long-Term Planning

While short-term analytics projects can offer quick wins, the true value of data analytics emerges when it is embedded in long-term planning. This approach requires an understanding of how current analytics efforts impact future objectives, as well as how data-driven insights can shape strategic initiatives. Ways to embed analytics in long-term planning include:

- **Forecasting and Trend Analysis**: Use predictive analytics to forecast future trends, market conditions, or customer preferences. Long-term forecasting supports planning around resources, investments, and strategic shifts.
- **Scenario Planning**: Scenario analysis helps organizations prepare for various outcomes by modeling different "what-if" scenarios. This approach enables companies to be more agile and responsive to market changes.
- **Continuous Learning and Adaptation**: Data analytics is not a one-time task; it requires regular updates and adjustments. Organizations that treat analytics as an

ongoing process are better equipped to adapt to emerging trends and refine strategies over time.

For example, a retail company could use trend analysis to predict seasonal demand fluctuations, planning inventory and staffing accordingly. By integrating this data into long-term plans, they not only improve efficiency but also enhance customer satisfaction through timely product availability.

4. Fostering Collaboration Between Analytics and Business Teams

To connect data analytics with strategic goals, there must be a bridge between analytics teams and business units. Collaboration ensures that analytics insights are relevant, actionable, and aligned with strategic objectives. Business leaders bring context and industry knowledge, while analysts provide the technical expertise needed to extract meaningful insights from data.

Strategies for fostering collaboration include:

- **Cross-Functional Teams**: Establish teams that include members from analytics, marketing, finance, and other departments. These teams work together on projects, ensuring that all perspectives are considered.
- **Regular Communication**: Encourage regular meetings between analytics teams and business units to discuss goals, review insights, and refine analytics projects.
- **Business Literacy for Analysts**: Equip analysts with a deep understanding of the business and its goals, enabling them to focus on data insights that drive strategic value.

For instance, in a retail organization, analysts working closely with the marketing team might develop customer segmentation models that align with marketing strategies, allowing for more targeted and effective campaigns.

5. Cultivating a Culture of Data-Driven Decision-Making

A data-driven culture ensures that decisions at every level of the organization are guided by evidence and analysis. When data-driven thinking is a part of the company's DNA, employees are more likely to embrace analytics insights and incorporate them into their daily decision-making.

Elements of a data-driven culture include:

- **Leadership Support**: Leaders should champion the use of data in decision-making, setting an example for others to follow.
- **Accessible Data**: Ensure that data is readily available and accessible to all departments, empowering employees to make data-informed decisions.
- **Training and Development**: Invest in data literacy training, helping employees understand and interpret data, even if they are not in analytics roles.
- **Celebrating Data Successes**: Highlight examples of data-driven success, reinforcing the value of analytics in achieving business outcomes.

Creating a data-driven culture encourages employees to think analytically and base their actions on evidence, creating a unified approach to reaching strategic goals.

6. Measuring the Impact of Data Analytics on Strategic Goals

Measuring the impact of data analytics initiatives is essential for validating their contribution to strategic goals. By assessing the outcomes of analytics projects, organizations can identify areas of success, adjust their approaches, and optimize future efforts.

Ways to measure impact include:

- **Comparing KPIs Before and After Analytics Projects**: Analyze changes in key metrics, such as customer retention rates or cost savings, to gauge the effectiveness of data-driven decisions.
- **Calculating Return on Investment (ROI)**: Evaluate the financial return of analytics initiatives relative to their cost, providing a quantifiable measure of value.
- **Conducting Case Studies**: Documenting case studies of successful analytics projects offers insights into how analytics contributed to business objectives, serving as examples for future efforts.

For instance, a logistics company implementing predictive analytics to optimize delivery routes might measure the reduction in fuel costs and delivery times, demonstrating the tangible benefits of data-driven decision-making.

Conclusion

Connecting data analytics to strategic goals and long-term business objectives is essential for deriving true value from data. By aligning analytics initiatives with key performance indicators, embedding data-driven thinking into long-term planning, fostering cross-functional collaboration, and cultivating a data-driven culture, organizations can ensure that analytics efforts support the broader mission and vision of the company. This approach enables companies to not only react to immediate challenges but also proactively shape their future, ensuring sustained growth and success in an increasingly data-driven world. As you move forward, this foundation of aligning analytics with strategy will be critical for unlocking the full potential of data-driven insights and achieving meaningful impact.

Techniques for Aligning Analytics with Decision-Making to Drive Impact

Incorporating analytics into decision-making processes is a powerful way to enhance organizational performance, predict market changes, and make evidence-based choices that support strategic goals. However, simply having data and insights is not enough. To maximize the impact of analytics, it's essential to align these insights with decision-making frameworks that guide business actions. In this section, we'll explore proven techniques for integrating analytics into decision-making processes to ensure that insights are not only actionable but also impactful.

1. Translating Data into Actionable Insights

Raw data and even well-crafted reports mean little without a clear path to action. Translating data into actionable insights involves making complex data understandable and directly linking it to business goals. This process requires both technical skill and the ability to communicate insights effectively to decision-makers.

Steps to make data actionable include:

- **Summarizing Key Findings**: Distill data into clear, concise insights that are directly relevant to the decision at hand. Use visualization tools, dashboards, and summary reports to make complex data accessible.
- **Highlighting Trends and Patterns**: Point out trends that indicate emerging opportunities or risks, focusing on how these insights relate to business goals.
- **Providing Clear Recommendations**: Go beyond presenting data; suggest specific actions that decision-makers can take. When possible, offer a range of options, such as high-impact but resource-intensive actions alongside lower-cost alternatives.

For example, if an e-commerce business sees a trend of high cart abandonment rates, actionable insights might include identifying at which stage users drop off and recommending interventions like checkout simplification or targeted discount campaigns.

2. Embedding Analytics into Decision-Making Frameworks

To make analytics part of everyday decision-making, organizations should embed analytics into structured decision-making frameworks, such as SWOT analysis (Strengths, Weaknesses, Opportunities, Threats) or KPI-driven scorecards. This approach formalizes the use of data in evaluating options and making choices.

Embedding analytics in decision-making frameworks can involve:

- **Integrating KPIs and Benchmarks**: Use relevant KPIs and industry benchmarks as metrics in decision-making frameworks. For instance, during a SWOT analysis, quantitative metrics can highlight strengths and weaknesses in specific areas, such as customer satisfaction or operational efficiency.

- **Creating Data-Driven Scorecards**: Scorecards provide a structured way to evaluate decisions based on performance metrics. By incorporating analytics directly into these scorecards, leaders can objectively assess options.
- **Developing Data-Driven Business Cases**: Whenever possible, support major decisions with data-driven business cases that show potential ROI, projected impact, and alignment with long-term goals.

For instance, a healthcare organization using a data-driven SWOT analysis could evaluate a new patient management system. They might assess "strengths" by examining improved patient outcomes from similar systems, "weaknesses" by identifying costs, "opportunities" through expected efficiencies, and "threats" by anticipating implementation challenges.

3. Prioritizing High-Impact Analytics Projects

Not all analytics projects have the same potential for impact. Prioritizing projects that are most likely to influence critical business outcomes ensures that resources are allocated effectively and results are maximized.

Techniques for prioritizing high-impact analytics projects include:

- **Impact vs. Effort Matrix**: An impact-effort matrix helps determine which analytics projects offer the most value relative to their difficulty. Projects that are high-impact but low-effort should be prioritized, while high-effort, low-impact projects may be deferred.

- **Focus on Business Objectives**: Evaluate each project based on how well it supports key business goals, such as increasing market share, improving customer satisfaction, or reducing operational costs.
- **Quick Wins and Long-Term Investments**: Identify quick-win projects that can deliver immediate value alongside longer-term projects that support strategic growth. This balance allows analytics teams to show results quickly while working on high-impact initiatives.

For example, a financial institution might prioritize analytics projects that focus on fraud detection (high impact, quick win) while also investing in a longer-term project to improve predictive models for customer retention.

4. Scenario Analysis and Forecasting to Inform Decision-Making

Scenario analysis and forecasting enable organizations to evaluate potential future conditions and make proactive decisions. By modeling different scenarios, decision-makers can anticipate how various factors, such as economic shifts or competitive pressures, might impact the organization. This foresight allows companies to adapt more quickly and make informed decisions even in uncertain environments.

To leverage scenario analysis and forecasting:

- **Develop Multiple Scenarios**: Create best-case, worst-case, and most likely scenarios based on available data.

This approach helps decision-makers consider a range of possibilities.

- **Identify Key Drivers**: Focus on key factors that influence outcomes, such as customer demand, market conditions, or supply chain stability. Understanding these drivers enables more accurate forecasts.
- **Test Decisions Against Scenarios**: Evaluate potential actions against each scenario to see how they would perform under different conditions. This exercise can reveal both risks and opportunities, allowing leaders to make more resilient decisions.

For example, a logistics company might use scenario analysis to model the impact of fuel price fluctuations on delivery costs. This insight allows them to plan for contingencies, such as adjusting routes or partnering with alternative suppliers.

5. Establishing Feedback Loops for Continuous Improvement

Continuous improvement is essential for maximizing the impact of analytics on decision-making. By establishing feedback loops, organizations can monitor the outcomes of data-driven decisions, learn from results, and refine their approaches over time.

Key components of effective feedback loops include:

- **Performance Monitoring**: Track KPIs and other metrics that indicate whether a decision is achieving the desired outcomes. Regular monitoring helps identify areas that need adjustment.

- **Iterative Testing**: For decisions with multiple potential actions, consider A/B testing or pilot programs to evaluate effectiveness. This iterative approach allows organizations to learn and adapt before full-scale implementation.
- **Learning and Adaptation**: Use insights from feedback loops to refine analytics processes, improve accuracy, and enhance alignment with strategic goals.

For instance, an online retailer implementing a new recommendation engine could monitor customer engagement metrics like click-through rates and purchase frequency. This data helps them adjust recommendations over time, enhancing both customer experience and revenue.

6. Communicating Analytics Insights Effectively to Drive Decision-Making

The value of analytics insights depends not only on their accuracy but also on how effectively they are communicated to decision-makers. Communicating insights in a clear, compelling manner is crucial for driving impact, ensuring that leaders understand the data and its implications.

Techniques for effective communication include:

- **Tailoring the Message to the Audience**: Customize the presentation of insights based on the audience's knowledge level and needs. Executives may need a high-level summary, while technical teams benefit from detailed analysis.

- **Using Data Visualization**: Visual aids, such as charts and graphs, make complex data more accessible, highlighting key trends and insights.
- **Storytelling with Data**: Frame data insights as part of a broader story, connecting insights to business goals and real-world implications. Data storytelling helps decision-makers see the relevance of insights and envision their impact.

For example, a data analyst presenting to the executive team might use a combination of high-level dashboards and storytelling to show how a new customer segmentation strategy could improve market penetration and customer loyalty.

Conclusion

Aligning analytics with decision-making is essential for organizations seeking to leverage data for strategic impact. By translating data into actionable insights, embedding analytics into decision-making frameworks, prioritizing high-impact projects, using scenario analysis, establishing feedback loops, and communicating effectively, companies can maximize the value of analytics in achieving business objectives. These techniques create a systematic approach to incorporating analytics into decision-making, empowering organizations to not only understand what the data says but also to act on it decisively and strategically. As we proceed through the book, each chapter will build on these foundational techniques, exploring advanced strategies for integrating analytics with organizational decision-making.

Chapter 3: Machine Learning Fundamentals for Advanced Analysts

Introduction to Essential Machine Learning Algorithms and When to Use Each

Machine learning has become a cornerstone of data-driven decision-making, enabling organizations to make predictions, automate processes, and uncover patterns that might otherwise go unnoticed. However, the power of machine learning depends on choosing the right algorithm for the task. Each algorithm is designed to tackle specific types of problems, from classification and regression to clustering and anomaly detection. This chapter provides an overview of essential machine learning algorithms, explaining when to use each and the types of problems they are best suited to solve.

1. Supervised Learning: Leveraging Labeled Data for Prediction

Supervised learning algorithms are trained on labeled data, meaning that each input in the training dataset is paired with the correct output. These algorithms are commonly used for tasks where the goal is to predict an outcome based on input data, such as classifying an email as spam or non-spam, predicting stock prices, or identifying fraudulent transactions.

Key supervised learning algorithms include:

- **Linear Regression**: Linear regression is a foundational algorithm used for predicting continuous values, such as sales forecasts or pricing trends. It assumes a linear relationship between the input variables and the output, making it simple but effective for many real-world applications.

- When to Use: Use linear regression when the relationship between variables is approximately linear, and the goal is to predict a continuous outcome.

- **Logistic Regression**: Despite its name, logistic regression is used for classification tasks. It is particularly useful for binary classification, such as determining whether a customer will make a purchase (yes/no) or if a patient has a certain disease (yes/no).

  - When to Use: Choose logistic regression when you have a binary classification problem and need interpretable results.

- **Decision Trees**: Decision trees are versatile algorithms that can be used for both classification and regression tasks. They split data into subsets based on feature values, forming a tree structure that is easy to interpret.

  - When to Use: Decision trees are ideal for cases where interpretability is important, such as in credit scoring or medical diagnosis. They work well with both categorical and continuous data.

- **Random Forest**: Random forest is an ensemble algorithm that combines multiple decision trees to improve accuracy and reduce overfitting. By averaging the predictions of several trees, random forests achieve more robust results than individual decision trees.

o **When to Use**: Random forest is suitable for complex classification and regression problems where accuracy is prioritized over interpretability.

- **Support Vector Machines (SVM)**: SVMs are powerful algorithms used for classification and regression, particularly effective in cases where the data is not linearly separable. SVMs create a hyperplane to separate data into different classes, maximizing the margin between them.

  o **When to Use**: Use SVM when you have high-dimensional data or non-linear relationships, such as in image recognition or text classification.

- **k-Nearest Neighbors (k-NN)**: k-NN is a simple algorithm that classifies data points based on the majority class of their nearest neighbors. It works well with smaller datasets and requires little training, as it stores all training data and calculates similarities during classification.

  o **When to Use**: k-NN is useful for classification tasks in smaller datasets or when interpretability is essential. It's often used in recommendation systems and anomaly detection.

2. Unsupervised Learning: Discovering Patterns Without Labeled Data

Unsupervised learning algorithms work with unlabeled data, focusing on discovering patterns, structures, or clusters within the dataset. These algorithms are ideal for tasks like customer segmentation, anomaly detection, and dimensionality reduction.

Key unsupervised learning algorithms include:

- **k-Means Clustering**: k-Means is a popular clustering algorithm that partitions data into a specified number of clusters (k) based on similarity. Each data point is assigned to the nearest cluster centroid, creating distinct groups within the data.
  - o **When to Use**: k-Means is suitable for clustering tasks where the number of clusters is known or can be estimated, such as customer segmentation.
- **Hierarchical Clustering**: Hierarchical clustering creates a tree of clusters, organizing data into a hierarchy of nested groups. Unlike k-means, it does not require the number of clusters to be specified in advance.
  - o **When to Use**: Use hierarchical clustering when you need a hierarchy of clusters or are uncertain about the optimal number of clusters, such as in gene expression analysis.
- **Principal Component Analysis (PCA)**: PCA is a dimensionality reduction technique that transforms data into a lower-dimensional space while preserving variance. It is used for simplifying datasets with many features, reducing computational complexity, and avoiding overfitting.

o **When to Use**: PCA is useful for data visualization, noise reduction, and when working with high-dimensional datasets in applications like image compression or exploratory data analysis.

- **Anomaly Detection (e.g., Isolation Forest)**: Anomaly detection algorithms are used to identify unusual data points or outliers within a dataset. Isolation forests are commonly used for detecting anomalies in large datasets by isolating data points in a tree structure.

  o **When to Use**: Use anomaly detection algorithms when identifying rare or unusual events, such as fraud detection or network intrusion.

3. Semi-Supervised Learning: Combining Labeled and Unlabeled Data

Semi-supervised learning algorithms work with a mix of labeled and unlabeled data, which is useful in cases where labeled data is limited but unlabeled data is abundant. These algorithms use the labeled data to inform their understanding of the unlabeled data, achieving better performance than unsupervised learning alone.

- **Self-Training and Co-Training Algorithms**: Self-training and co-training are approaches where the model iteratively labels the unlabeled data based on predictions made by the labeled data. Self-training uses one model, while co-training employs multiple models to improve label accuracy.

○ **When to Use**: Semi-supervised learning is useful when labeling data is expensive or time-consuming, such as in medical imaging or speech recognition.

4. Reinforcement Learning: Decision-Making Through Trial and Error

Reinforcement learning (RL) involves training an agent to make decisions by interacting with an environment. Through a system of rewards and penalties, the agent learns to take actions that maximize cumulative rewards. RL is commonly used in applications that require dynamic decision-making and long-term planning.

- **Q-Learning**: Q-Learning is a popular RL algorithm where the agent learns a Q-function, which estimates the expected utility of actions in given states. It's suitable for discrete action spaces.
  - ○ **When to Use**: Q-Learning is ideal for problems with well-defined states and actions, such as games or robotic pathfinding.
- **Deep Q-Networks (DQN)**: DQN combines deep learning with Q-learning, enabling it to handle high-dimensional input spaces, such as image-based environments.
  - ○ **When to Use**: DQN is useful for complex environments where actions are continuous or involve large state spaces, like autonomous driving or advanced gaming applications.

5. Ensemble Methods: Combining Models for Improved Performance

Ensemble methods combine multiple algorithms to improve overall model accuracy and robustness. By aggregating the predictions of several models, ensembles reduce the risk of overfitting and improve generalization.

- **Bagging (Bootstrap Aggregating)**: Bagging trains multiple models independently on different subsets of the data, then aggregates their predictions. Random forest is a common example.
  - o **When to Use**: Use bagging to reduce variance in high-variance models, especially in noisy datasets.
- **Boosting**: Boosting trains multiple models sequentially, where each model attempts to correct the errors of the previous one. Algorithms like AdaBoost and Gradient Boosting are popular in this category.
  - o **When to Use**: Boosting is ideal for reducing bias and increasing accuracy, particularly in complex datasets with nonlinear relationships.

6. Neural Networks and Deep Learning: Handling High-Complexity Data

Neural networks are highly flexible algorithms inspired by the human brain, capable of handling complex data like images, text, and sound. Deep learning extends neural networks to multiple layers, allowing for more sophisticated modeling of high-dimensional data.

- **Convolutional Neural Networks (CNNs)**: CNNs are specialized for image data, using convolutional layers to capture spatial features and patterns.

- o **When to Use**: Use CNNs for image recognition, object detection, and visual processing tasks.
- **Recurrent Neural Networks (RNNs)**: RNNs are suited for sequential data, as they maintain memory of previous inputs. They are commonly used in natural language processing and time-series analysis.
  - o **When to Use**: RNNs are ideal for language translation, speech recognition, and financial forecasting.

Conclusion

Understanding the essential machine learning algorithms and their applications is critical for any advanced analyst. Each algorithm has strengths and limitations, making it suitable for specific tasks within supervised, unsupervised, semi-supervised, reinforcement learning, ensemble methods, and deep learning. By choosing the right algorithm for each problem, analysts can leverage the power of machine learning to deliver actionable insights, automate decision-making, and drive strategic impact. In the following chapters, we will explore practical examples and advanced techniques that will build upon this foundation, enabling you to apply these algorithms effectively in real-world analytics.

In-Depth Coverage of Supervised, Unsupervised, and Reinforcement Learning with Examples

Machine learning is built on three primary types of learning paradigms: supervised, unsupervised, and reinforcement learning. Each approach is designed to handle specific kinds of problems, data structures, and goals. This chapter dives deeply into each type, providing examples that illustrate their real-world applications, strengths, and best use cases.

1. Supervised Learning: Learning from Labeled Data

Supervised learning is a structured approach where models learn from labeled datasets. In this setting, each input has a corresponding output, allowing the algorithm to find patterns that link inputs to outputs. Supervised learning is used primarily for classification and regression tasks where predicting known outcomes is essential.

Supervised Learning Algorithms

Some common supervised learning algorithms include:

- **Linear Regression**: Used to predict a continuous output based on input variables. Linear regression models a linear relationship between variables and is often used in pricing models or demand forecasting.

- **Logistic Regression**: Despite its name, logistic regression is used for classification. It outputs probabilities for binary outcomes, making it ideal for binary classification problems like predicting customer churn or whether an email is spam.

- **Decision Trees**: Decision trees are intuitive models that split data into branches based on decision rules. These rules allow decision trees to classify data based on known input characteristics.

- **Support Vector Machines (SVM)**: SVMs are powerful classifiers that find the best boundary (hyperplane) that separates classes, especially useful in high-dimensional spaces.

Example of Supervised Learning

Predicting Loan Default

Consider a bank that wants to predict whether a borrower will default on a loan. The bank can use historical data on previous borrowers, including labeled data indicating who defaulted and who repaid their loan. Using supervised learning, the bank trains a model (e.g., a decision tree) on this dataset, with features such as borrower income, credit score, and loan amount. Once trained, the model can predict whether a new borrower is likely to default based on similar features, helping the bank make more informed lending decisions.

2. Unsupervised Learning: Discovering Patterns in Unlabeled Data

Unsupervised learning works with datasets that lack labeled outputs. The goal is to uncover hidden patterns, clusters, or structures within the data. This type of learning is useful for tasks such as customer segmentation, anomaly detection, and feature reduction, where the goal is to make sense of data without predefined categories or classes.

Unsupervised Learning Algorithms

Popular unsupervised learning algorithms include:

- **k-Means Clustering**: A simple but effective algorithm that groups data into k clusters based on similarity. Each data point belongs to the nearest cluster centroid.
- **Hierarchical Clustering**: Builds a hierarchy of clusters, creating a tree-like structure where similar clusters are

nested within larger ones. It's useful for discovering hierarchical relationships within data.

- **Principal Component Analysis (PCA)**: A dimensionality reduction technique that reduces the number of features in a dataset while preserving the most important information, making it useful for simplifying high-dimensional data.
- **Anomaly Detection (Isolation Forest, One-Class SVM)**: These algorithms identify unusual or rare patterns, commonly used in fraud detection or quality control.

Example of Unsupervised Learning

Customer Segmentation for E-commerce

An e-commerce company wants to segment its customers based on their purchasing behavior to create targeted marketing strategies. Since there is no predefined label for "type of customer," the company uses an unsupervised algorithm like k-means clustering. The model analyzes purchase frequency, average spending, and product preferences, grouping customers into segments based on these patterns. Each segment represents a group with similar behaviors, such as "frequent buyers" or "price-sensitive shoppers," allowing the company to tailor its marketing to each group's preferences.

3. Reinforcement Learning: Learning Through Trial and Error

Reinforcement learning (RL) is a unique approach where an agent learns to make decisions by interacting with an environment and receiving feedback in the form of rewards or penalties. Unlike supervised and unsupervised learning, RL focuses on sequential decision-making, where actions taken in the present influence outcomes in the future. This trial-and-error approach allows the agent to learn strategies that maximize long-term rewards.

Reinforcement Learning Algorithms

Common reinforcement learning algorithms include:

- **Q-Learning**: A model-free algorithm that uses a Q-table to estimate the expected rewards of actions in given states. The agent updates its Q-values as it learns, seeking actions that maximize rewards.
- **Deep Q-Networks (DQN)**: Combines Q-learning with deep learning to handle complex environments with high-dimensional state spaces, such as image-based inputs. DQNs enable RL in scenarios where a simple Q-table would be insufficient.
- **Policy Gradient Methods**: These algorithms, like REINFORCE or Actor-Critic methods, learn policies directly, optimizing the probability of taking actions that yield high rewards. They are suitable for continuous action spaces.

Example of Reinforcement Learning

Autonomous Driving

An example of reinforcement learning in action is autonomous driving. Here, an RL agent (the car) interacts with the environment (the road and traffic) and receives feedback based on its actions, such as staying within lanes, avoiding collisions, or obeying traffic signals. The agent receives positive rewards for safe driving behaviors and penalties for dangerous actions. Over time, the RL agent learns an optimal driving policy, adapting to different traffic scenarios and improving its ability to drive safely and efficiently.

In-Depth Analysis of Each Learning Paradigm

A. Supervised Learning: Advantages and Limitations

Supervised learning excels when there is a clear relationship between input features and the target variable. Its predictive power makes it valuable in scenarios where the goal is to classify or predict outcomes. However, it requires labeled data, which can be costly and time-consuming to obtain. Additionally, supervised learning may struggle with complex patterns if the relationship between inputs and outputs is not linear or straightforward.

Strengths:
- High accuracy with labeled data.
- Well-suited for predictive tasks with clear outcomes.

Limitations:
- Dependency on labeled data.
- Risk of overfitting in complex models with small datasets.

B. Unsupervised Learning: Flexibility and Challenges

Unsupervised learning is advantageous when data lacks labels or predefined categories, enabling analysts to explore and discover patterns organically. It is particularly useful for exploratory analysis, reducing dimensionality, and clustering. However, results may be harder to interpret, as unsupervised algorithms do not provide clear labels, and it can be challenging to validate the quality of clusters or groups.

Strengths:
- Useful for exploratory data analysis.
- Capable of identifying hidden structures.

Limitations:
- Lack of labeled data can make interpretation difficult.
- Clustering results may be sensitive to initial parameter choices (e.g., number of clusters).

C. Reinforcement Learning: Dynamic Decision-Making with High Complexity

Reinforcement learning is unique in its ability to optimize actions over time, making it ideal for dynamic environments where decision-making is ongoing. RL's feedback-based system enables agents to learn complex behaviors in interactive settings. However, RL models are computationally intensive and require large amounts of training data, especially in complex environments with high-dimensional states or continuous action spaces.

Strengths:
- Effective for complex, interactive environments.
- Optimizes long-term strategies.

Limitations:
- High computational cost and training time.
- Requires well-defined rewards and penalties.

Conclusion

Supervised, unsupervised, and reinforcement learning represent the three pillars of machine learning, each tailored to specific types of tasks and challenges. Supervised learning excels at prediction with labeled data, unsupervised learning reveals patterns in unlabeled data, and reinforcement learning is ideal for interactive, dynamic environments. By understanding when and how to use each learning paradigm, advanced analysts can apply machine learning to a wide array of real-world problems, creating robust solutions that drive value across industries. As we continue, we will explore more complex applications and techniques, building upon this foundation to tackle sophisticated analytics challenges.

Chapter 4: Data Mining Techniques: Uncovering Hidden Patterns and Trends

Comprehensive Exploration of Clustering, Association Rules, Anomaly Detection, and More

Data mining is the process of discovering meaningful patterns, relationships, and trends within large datasets. By identifying these hidden insights, organizations can make data-driven decisions, optimize operations, and reveal opportunities that would otherwise go unnoticed. This chapter explores essential data mining techniques, including clustering, association rules, anomaly detection, and others, providing a comprehensive toolkit for uncovering hidden patterns in data.

1. Clustering: Grouping Data into Meaningful Segments

Clustering is an unsupervised learning technique that groups data points into clusters based on similarity. Unlike classification, clustering does not rely on labeled data. Instead, it discovers natural groupings within the data, making it useful for customer segmentation, image processing, and identifying similar patterns.

Popular Clustering Algorithms

- **k-Means Clustering**: The k-means algorithm partitions data into k clusters, where each data point belongs to the nearest cluster centroid. The algorithm iteratively adjusts the centroids to minimize variance within each cluster.
    - **Application**: k-means is widely used for customer segmentation, where it groups

customers with similar purchasing behavior, enabling personalized marketing campaigns.

- **Hierarchical Clustering**: This algorithm creates a hierarchy of clusters, using either a top-down (divisive) or bottom-up (agglomerative) approach. The result is a tree-like structure, or dendrogram, that reveals nested groupings.
  - o **Application**: Hierarchical clustering is useful for scenarios where relationships between clusters are important, such as in genetic research or text analysis.
- **DBSCAN (Density-Based Spatial Clustering of Applications with Noise)**: DBSCAN groups data points based on density, identifying clusters of varying shapes and sizes while marking outliers. Unlike k-means, it doesn't require specifying the number of clusters.
  - o **Application**: DBSCAN is used in geospatial analysis to identify clusters in satellite images or geographic data, especially when there is noise or varying cluster densities.

Example of Clustering

Customer Segmentation in Retail

A retail company wants to better understand its customer base to enhance marketing efforts. By applying k-means clustering on data like purchase history, age, and location, the company segments customers into clusters (e.g., "frequent buyers," "price-sensitive shoppers"). This insight allows them to tailor their marketing campaigns to different customer needs and improve engagement.

2. Association Rule Mining: Discovering Relationships Between Variables

Association rule mining uncovers relationships, or associations, between items in large datasets. The technique identifies rules that reveal how items or events are related, typically in the form of "if-then" statements. Association rules are frequently used in market basket analysis, where the goal is to find patterns in customer purchases.

Key Concepts in Association Rule Mining

- **Support**: The frequency of an itemset appearing in a dataset. High support indicates that a rule is common in the data.
- **Confidence**: The likelihood of an item appearing if another item is present. Confidence measures the strength of the association.
- **Lift**: The ratio of observed support to expected support if items were independent. Lift values greater than 1 indicate a positive association between items.

Algorithm for Association Rule Mining

- **Apriori Algorithm**: The Apriori algorithm generates frequent itemsets by identifying subsets with high support. It then calculates confidence and lift to generate association rules.
  - **Application**: The Apriori algorithm is widely used in market basket analysis to identify which products are frequently purchased together,

enabling strategies like cross-selling and product bundling.

Example of Association Rule Mining

Market Basket Analysis in E-commerce

An online retailer analyzes transaction data to discover associations between items frequently bought together. Using Apriori, they find that customers who purchase coffee makers also buy coffee filters. With this insight, the retailer can bundle these items or recommend them during checkout, boosting sales and customer satisfaction.

3. Anomaly Detection: Identifying Unusual Patterns in Data

Anomaly detection identifies rare, out-of-the-ordinary data points that differ significantly from the majority of the data. These anomalies, or outliers, can represent unusual events like fraud, equipment failures, or data errors. Anomaly detection is critical in industries where such events have significant consequences, such as finance, cybersecurity, and manufacturing.

Anomaly Detection Algorithms

- **Isolation Forest**: This algorithm isolates anomalies by randomly selecting features and splitting data points along feature values. Anomalies are easier to isolate, requiring fewer splits. Isolation forests are fast and work well with large datasets.
  - ○ **Application**: Isolation forests are commonly used in fraud detection, where they identify suspicious transactions that deviate from typical patterns.

- **One-Class SVM**: The One-Class Support Vector Machine (SVM) is a supervised anomaly detection algorithm that finds a boundary around normal data points, treating any point outside this boundary as an anomaly.
  - o **Application**: One-Class SVM is suitable for network security, identifying unusual activity that might indicate unauthorized access.
- **Autoencoders**: In deep learning, autoencoders are neural networks that learn to compress and reconstruct data. Anomalies are identified when data points cannot be accurately reconstructed, suggesting they deviate from the normal pattern.
  - o **Application**: Autoencoders are used in industries like manufacturing, where they detect machine faults by analyzing deviations in sensor data.

Example of Anomaly Detection

Fraud Detection in Banking

A bank uses anomaly detection to monitor transactions for unusual activity that may indicate fraud. By training an isolation forest on normal transaction patterns, the model can detect anomalies, such as unusually large withdrawals or international purchases, and flag these for further review. This proactive approach helps prevent financial losses due to fraud.

4. Dimensionality Reduction: Simplifying Complex Datasets

Dimensionality reduction reduces the number of features in a dataset while preserving essential information. It is particularly useful in high-dimensional datasets, where many features can make analysis slow, complex, or prone to overfitting. Techniques like PCA and t-SNE (t-distributed stochastic neighbor embedding) are commonly used for dimensionality reduction.

Dimensionality Reduction Techniques

- **Principal Component Analysis (PCA)**: PCA transforms data into a lower-dimensional space by projecting it onto principal components, which capture the highest variance. PCA is widely used to simplify datasets for visualization and analysis.
  - ○ **Application**: PCA is applied in fields like image processing, where it reduces the dimensionality of images for faster computation without significant loss of information.
- **t-SNE**: This technique is primarily used for visualizing high-dimensional data by mapping it to a lower-dimensional space. t-SNE preserves local similarities, making it ideal for clustering visualizations.
  - ○ **Application**: t-SNE is often used in bioinformatics to visualize gene expression data, revealing natural groupings and patterns.

Example of Dimensionality Reduction

Data Simplification in Marketing Analytics

A marketing analytics team analyzes customer behavior data with hundreds of features, from demographic data to online browsing habits. Using PCA, they reduce the dataset to a smaller number of principal components, making the data easier to visualize and analyze while still capturing key patterns. This reduced dataset helps the team identify broad customer trends without getting lost in excessive detail.

5. Text Mining: Extracting Insights from Unstructured Text
Text mining is a subfield of data mining that focuses on analyzing and extracting meaningful patterns from unstructured text data. With the rise of digital communication, text mining has become essential for analyzing customer feedback, social media, and reviews.

Text Mining Techniques
- **Natural Language Processing (NLP)**: NLP techniques enable computers to understand and analyze human language. NLP techniques include tokenization, stemming, sentiment analysis, and named entity recognition.
    - o **Application**: NLP is used for sentiment analysis in social media monitoring, where companies analyze public sentiment toward their brand.
- **Topic Modeling (LDA)**: Latent Dirichlet Allocation (LDA) is a popular topic modeling technique that uncovers topics within a collection of documents, making it useful for organizing and summarizing large volumes of text.
    - o **Application**: LDA is used in content recommendation systems, where it categorizes articles or products into relevant topics for users.

Example of Text Mining
Sentiment Analysis for Brand Monitoring

A company monitors customer sentiment across social media to gauge public perception of its brand. Using NLP techniques, the company identifies trends in sentiment, such as positive or negative feedback on new products. This analysis helps the company respond to customer needs and enhance brand reputation.

6. Time Series Analysis: Identifying Patterns Over Time

Time series analysis focuses on data points collected or recorded over time. This technique identifies trends, seasonality, and cyclic patterns within time-dependent data, making it ideal for forecasting and trend analysis.

Time Series Analysis Techniques

- **ARIMA (AutoRegressive Integrated Moving Average)**: ARIMA models time series data by combining autoregressive and moving average elements, making it useful for short-term forecasting.
  - ○ **Application**: ARIMA is commonly used in finance for predicting stock prices and in sales forecasting.
- **Exponential Smoothing**: This technique smooths data by giving more weight to recent observations, helping identify trends and seasonality.
  - ○ **Application**: Exponential smoothing is used for demand forecasting in supply chain management, where accurate predictions are essential for inventory planning.

Example of Time Series Analysis

Energy Consumption Forecasting

A utility company uses time series analysis to forecast energy consumption for the coming months. By analyzing historical energy usage data with ARIMA, the company identifies seasonal peaks and trends. This forecasting enables the company to prepare for periods of high demand, ensuring reliable service for customers.

Case Studies on Using Data Mining for Customer Segmentation, Fraud Detection, and Recommendation Engines

Data mining provides powerful techniques for extracting valuable insights from large datasets, transforming raw information into actionable strategies across industries. In this chapter, we'll delve into real-world case studies that demonstrate how companies leverage data mining to address key challenges such as customer segmentation, fraud detection, and personalized recommendations. These examples illustrate the process, techniques, and impact of data mining in driving business success.

1. Customer Segmentation in Retail: Targeted Marketing and Personalization

Customer segmentation is a critical application of data mining that allows companies to understand and target different groups within their customer base. By grouping customers based on shared characteristics, businesses can tailor their marketing efforts, improve customer satisfaction, and increase sales.

Case Study: Retail Store's Data-Driven Marketing Strategy

A large retail chain sought to improve the effectiveness of its marketing campaigns by identifying distinct customer segments based on shopping behavior and demographics. Using k-means clustering, the company analyzed data from thousands of customers, including purchase history, average spend, frequency of visits, and demographic factors such as age and income.

Data Mining Process

1. **Data Collection**: The company collected data from loyalty programs, in-store transactions, and online purchase histories.
2. **Feature Selection**: Key features included frequency of purchase, average transaction value, preferred product categories, and customer demographics.
3. **Clustering with k-Means**: By applying the k-means clustering algorithm, the company segmented customers into four primary clusters: high-frequency buyers, seasonal shoppers, bargain hunters, and high-spend loyalists.

Results and Impact

Each cluster revealed unique behaviors and preferences. For example, high-frequency buyers showed a preference for essential items, while seasonal shoppers were more responsive to holiday promotions. The company used these insights to create targeted marketing campaigns, offering personalized promotions to each segment. The result was a 20% increase in customer engagement and a 15% boost in campaign ROI, demonstrating the value of data mining in enhancing customer targeting and personalization.

2. Fraud Detection in Banking: Identifying Anomalous Transactions

Fraud detection is another crucial application of data mining, especially in sectors like finance where unauthorized transactions can lead to significant losses. By identifying anomalies in transaction patterns, financial institutions can flag suspicious activities for further investigation, protecting both their customers and their assets.

Case Study: A Bank's Approach to Transaction Anomaly Detection

A major bank faced increasing challenges in detecting fraudulent transactions due to the rise in digital banking. The bank decided to use anomaly detection techniques to identify suspicious transactions based on historical data. By training a model with isolation forest algorithms, the bank could pinpoint unusual patterns and flag potential fraud in real-time.

Data Mining Process

1. **Data Collection**: The bank analyzed millions of transactions, focusing on transaction amount, frequency, location, time, and device type.
2. **Feature Engineering**: The team created additional features, such as the average transaction value for each customer, the distance between transaction locations, and the frequency of cross-border transactions.
3. **Anomaly Detection with Isolation Forest**: Using isolation forests, the model could isolate rare, unusual

transactions that deviated significantly from a customer's typical behavior.

Results and Impact

The anomaly detection model flagged transactions that showed unusual patterns, such as high-value purchases in foreign locations or rapid transactions from different locations. The bank's fraud team reviewed these transactions, confirming a significant number of cases as fraudulent. By implementing this system, the bank reduced fraud losses by 30% within the first six months and improved its fraud detection rate by 40%, providing a proactive solution that benefited both the bank and its customers.

3. Recommendation Engines in E-commerce: Personalized Shopping Experiences

Recommendation engines are a powerful data mining application in the e-commerce industry, enhancing user experience by suggesting products that align with a customer's preferences. These engines analyze user behavior and item characteristics to provide personalized recommendations, improving engagement and sales.

Case Study: E-commerce Platform's Personalized Recommendation System

A popular e-commerce platform aimed to increase sales by providing personalized recommendations to its users. The company implemented a recommendation engine using collaborative filtering and association rule mining to suggest items based on customer behavior and item relationships.

Data Mining Process

1. **Data Collection**: The platform collected data on user behavior, including clicks, purchase history, browsing patterns, and product ratings.
2. **Collaborative Filtering**: By analyzing similarities between users, collaborative filtering identified items that similar customers enjoyed. For example, customers with similar browsing histories or purchase behaviors were more likely to receive recommendations for similar products.
3. **Association Rule Mining**: The platform also used association rule mining (using the Apriori algorithm) to identify frequently co-purchased items, enabling effective cross-selling and bundling suggestions.

Results and Impact

The recommendation engine provided highly relevant product suggestions to users, leading to increased engagement and a higher average order value. The platform's personalized recommendations contributed to a 25% increase in customer conversion rates and a 30% boost in repeat purchases, proving the value of tailored shopping experiences. Additionally, the association rules allowed the platform to create product bundles, increasing cross-selling opportunities and further enhancing the shopping experience.

4. Predictive Maintenance in Manufacturing: Reducing Downtime and Costs

In manufacturing, data mining techniques can help predict equipment failures before they occur, allowing companies to schedule maintenance proactively and reduce costly downtime.

Predictive maintenance leverages anomaly detection and time series analysis to monitor equipment health and detect signs of wear and tear.

Case Study: Industrial Plant's Predictive Maintenance Initiative

An industrial plant producing heavy machinery wanted to reduce unexpected equipment failures, which led to costly production stoppages. By implementing a predictive maintenance system, the company could analyze sensor data in real-time, using anomaly detection to identify early signs of equipment malfunction.

Data Mining Process

1. **Data Collection**: The plant collected sensor data, such as temperature, vibration, and pressure readings, from each machine in the facility.
2. **Time Series Analysis and Feature Engineering**: The team used time series analysis to track sensor readings over time and engineered features like rolling averages and moving variances to monitor equipment health.
3. **Anomaly Detection with Autoencoders**: An autoencoder, a neural network model, was used to learn typical sensor patterns. When sensor readings deviated significantly from the norm, the system flagged these anomalies as potential indicators of equipment failure.

Results and Impact

The predictive maintenance system successfully detected early signs of wear and tear, allowing the plant to schedule repairs before breakdowns occurred. Over the course of one year, the plant reduced unexpected downtime by 40% and maintenance costs by 25%. These improvements translated to millions in savings, demonstrating the value of data mining in industrial applications.

Conclusion

These case studies highlight the versatility and impact of data mining techniques in solving real-world problems across industries. By leveraging clustering, anomaly detection, association rules, and recommendation engines, organizations can drive insights that improve customer engagement, protect against fraud, enhance operational efficiency, and deliver tailored experiences. As we continue, this foundation in data mining techniques will support the development of more complex applications, empowering analysts to unlock the full potential of data and drive strategic impact in their fields.

Practical Tips for Translating Patterns into Actionable Insights

Data mining techniques enable organizations to uncover valuable patterns and trends within their datasets, but the real value lies in transforming these findings into actionable insights that can drive decision-making and strategy. Translating data mining patterns into meaningful business actions requires a mix of analytical skills, strategic thinking, and effective communication. This chapter provides practical tips to help analysts convert raw patterns into insights that inform decisions and create measurable impact.

1. Start with Clear Objectives and Business Questions

The foundation of actionable insights begins with a clear understanding of the problem and objectives. Before diving into data mining, ensure that you have a well-defined question or goal that aligns with business priorities. This clarity will guide the analysis and help determine which patterns are most relevant.

Practical Tips:

- **Identify Key Business Objectives**: Start by collaborating with stakeholders to clarify the goals, such as increasing sales, reducing churn, or improving operational efficiency.
- **Define Specific Questions**: Break down broad objectives into focused questions. For example, instead of a general goal like "improve customer satisfaction," ask, "What factors are most correlated with high customer satisfaction ratings?"
- **Set Success Metrics**: Define how you will measure the success of the insights. Metrics like ROI, customer retention rates, or time savings help quantify the impact of the findings.

2. Prioritize Patterns that Align with Strategic Goals

Not all patterns uncovered through data mining will be relevant. Prioritize patterns that directly support strategic goals or address immediate business needs. By focusing on high-impact patterns, you can ensure that insights lead to meaningful, actionable outcomes.

Practical Tips:

- **Evaluate Patterns Against Goals**: Assess each discovered pattern based on its relevance to the original business question. For example, if the goal is to increase sales, patterns indicating customer purchasing behavior or seasonal trends are more valuable than less relevant patterns.
- **Consider Business Impact**: Prioritize patterns with the highest potential impact. Use an impact-effort matrix to identify low-effort, high-impact insights that can be acted upon quickly.
- **Look for Quick Wins**: Identify "quick win" insights that require minimal resources to implement and can produce immediate benefits. For example, a pattern showing a spike in website traffic after a specific type of post could lead to content adjustments that drive further engagement.

3. Use Visualization to Highlight Key Insights

Data visualization is a powerful tool for making patterns more understandable and compelling. Visuals can transform complex data into clear, intuitive stories that decision-makers can grasp quickly, facilitating faster and more informed decision-making.

Practical Tips:

- **Choose the Right Chart Type**: Select a visualization format that best represents the pattern. Use bar charts for comparing categories, line charts for trends over time, and scatter plots to show relationships.
- **Focus on Key Takeaways**: Highlight essential insights within the visuals, such as peaks, trends, or outliers. Use

annotations or color to draw attention to the most important elements.

- **Simplify Complex Data**: Break down complex datasets into digestible visuals. Avoid overcrowding charts with too many variables or data points, and present one main message per visual to maintain clarity.

4. Contextualize Patterns to Enhance Relevance

Patterns on their own may not be actionable until they are placed in context. Adding context—such as historical comparisons, industry benchmarks, or business cycles—helps translate patterns into insights that resonate with stakeholders and reflect real-world situations.

Practical Tips:

- **Use Comparative Benchmarks**: Compare patterns to historical data or industry benchmarks to assess their significance. For example, an increase in monthly sales may seem promising, but comparing it to industry growth rates could provide a clearer picture.

- **Consider External Factors**: Identify external influences that may affect the pattern, such as seasonal trends, economic shifts, or competitive changes. For example, an increase in retail sales during the holiday season may not indicate long-term growth.

- **Incorporate Business Cycles**: Align patterns with business cycles or known industry trends. Understanding the cyclical nature of certain patterns helps determine if the pattern is likely to repeat or requires immediate action.

5. Translate Insights into Specific Recommendations

To make insights actionable, it's crucial to move beyond reporting patterns and offer specific, data-backed recommendations. Recommendations should provide a clear path for implementation, outlining the actions necessary to capitalize on or address the discovered patterns.

Practical Tips:

- **Be Clear and Specific**: Avoid vague suggestions. Instead of saying, "focus on customer retention," provide concrete steps, such as "implement a loyalty program targeting customers with high purchase frequency but low engagement."
- **Align with Available Resources**: Ensure recommendations are feasible, considering budget, personnel, and time constraints. Suggest phased implementation if a large-scale change isn't feasible all at once.
- **Provide a Range of Options**: Offer multiple actions when possible, such as low-cost and high-impact alternatives. This allows stakeholders to select solutions that best fit their current capabilities and priorities.

6. Test Insights with Small-Scale Pilots

Before rolling out major changes based on insights, consider implementing small-scale pilots to test the effectiveness of your recommendations. Pilots allow you to validate insights, refine approaches, and gather additional data, reducing the risk of full-scale implementation.

Practical Tips:

- **Choose a Representative Sample**: Run pilots in a subset of the business that represents the larger organization, such as testing a marketing campaign on a specific customer segment.
- **Define Pilot Success Metrics**: Set clear success metrics for the pilot, such as increased conversion rates or improved customer feedback scores. Metrics provide an objective basis for deciding whether to proceed with full-scale implementation.
- **Iterate Based on Results**: Use feedback and data from the pilot to fine-tune recommendations. This iterative approach helps ensure that final actions are well-informed and likely to succeed.

7. Communicate Insights Effectively to Stakeholders

Effective communication is essential for turning insights into action. Insights must be presented in a way that resonates with stakeholders, addressing their concerns, aligning with their goals, and explaining the potential impact on the organization.

Practical Tips:

- **Tailor Communication to the Audience**: Present insights differently depending on the audience. Executives may need high-level summaries focused on business impact, while technical teams may benefit from a more detailed analysis.
- **Focus on Benefits and ROI**: Highlight the business benefits and expected ROI of following the recommendations. Explain how the insights can help

achieve specific goals, such as cost savings, increased revenue, or improved customer satisfaction.

- **Encourage Interactive Discussion**: Invite feedback and discussion to foster buy-in and address potential concerns. This approach ensures that stakeholders understand the insights and feel involved in the decision-making process.

8. Establish Feedback Loops to Monitor Results and Adapt

Actionable insights should be continuously monitored to measure their effectiveness and refine strategies over time. Establishing feedback loops allows teams to track the impact of their actions, adapt based on results, and evolve strategies as new patterns emerge.

Practical Tips:

- **Define Metrics for Success**: Clearly outline the metrics that will indicate the success of each action. For example, if the recommendation was to target customer retention, track metrics like churn rate, repeat purchases, and customer lifetime value.
- **Regularly Review Outcomes**: Schedule regular check-ins to assess the outcomes and make necessary adjustments. Use dashboards to provide real-time visibility into key metrics and progress.
- **Adapt Based on Findings**: Be prepared to iterate and improve actions based on feedback. If initial recommendations are not yielding the expected results, re-evaluate the data, refine insights, and try new approaches.

Conclusion

The process of translating patterns into actionable insights is as critical as the data mining itself. By following these practical steps—defining clear objectives, prioritizing high-impact patterns, using effective visualization, providing context, offering specific recommendations, testing with pilots, communicating insights, and establishing feedback loops—analysts can ensure that their findings are both relevant and impactful. These practices allow organizations to leverage data mining techniques not only to uncover hidden patterns but to drive tangible results that align with strategic objectives. As we move forward, these skills will serve as the foundation for more advanced data analysis and decision-making approaches.

Chapter 5: Feature Engineering and Selection for Machine Learning Success

Techniques for Crafting High-Impact Features and Reducing Dimensionality

Feature engineering and selection are essential steps in building high-performing machine learning models. High-quality features transform raw data into meaningful signals, boosting model accuracy, interpretability, and computational efficiency. This chapter covers key techniques for creating impactful features, reducing dimensionality, and selecting the best attributes to improve model success.

1. The Importance of Feature Engineering in Machine Learning

Feature engineering is the process of transforming raw data into features that better represent the underlying patterns needed for a machine learning model to make predictions. It involves creating, modifying, or combining variables to reveal valuable insights that are not immediately visible in the raw data. High-impact features can significantly improve model performance by providing clearer, more meaningful inputs.

Benefits of Effective Feature Engineering

- **Improved Model Accuracy**: Good features enhance a model's predictive accuracy by capturing essential patterns.
- **Reduced Complexity**: By transforming raw data, feature engineering simplifies complex relationships, making it easier for models to learn.

- **Enhanced Interpretability**: Well-crafted features offer clearer insights, helping users understand the patterns that drive predictions.

2. Techniques for Crafting High-Impact Features

Creating high-impact features requires an understanding of the data, domain knowledge, and creativity. Here are some essential feature engineering techniques used to extract valuable information:

a. Binning and Discretization

Binning involves grouping continuous values into intervals, converting them into categorical bins. Discretizing data can help simplify patterns and make relationships easier for the model to learn.

- **Example**: Age can be binned into categories like "18–25," "26–35," and so on. This approach is helpful when different age groups have distinct behaviors or trends.

b. Polynomial and Interaction Features

Generating polynomial and interaction terms allows the model to capture non-linear relationships between variables. Polynomial features involve raising variables to a power, while interaction features involve combining variables.

- **Example**: In predicting housing prices, interaction features such as "house age * square footage" might reveal relationships between house age and size that affect price.

c. Encoding Categorical Variables

Machine learning algorithms require numerical input, so categorical variables must be encoded. Common encoding methods include:

- **One-Hot Encoding**: Creates a new binary column for each category, where each column represents the presence (1) or absence (0) of a category.
- **Label Encoding**: Assigns each category a unique numerical value, useful for ordinal categories with an inherent order.

d. Time-Based Features

Time-based features are derived from date and time data. Extracting components such as day of the week, month, hour, or season helps capture trends and patterns related to time.

- **Example**: In retail data, creating features like "day of the week" and "holiday" may reveal trends in sales that vary with the calendar.

e. Aggregation and Statistical Features

Aggregation features provide summary statistics based on groups within the data, such as mean, sum, or count. These features help capture general trends across groups or time periods.

- **Example**: In customer data, the average purchase frequency or total spending over time can be an indicator of customer loyalty.

f. Text Features

For text data, features such as word counts, term frequency-inverse document frequency (TF-IDF), and sentiment scores help convert unstructured data into useful numeric representations.

- **Example**: Analyzing product reviews might involve creating features based on positive or negative sentiment scores to understand customer feedback.

3. Feature Selection: Choosing the Most Valuable Features

Feature selection is the process of identifying and retaining only the most relevant features from a dataset. Reducing dimensionality helps improve model performance, reduce overfitting, and enhance interpretability. Here are popular techniques for effective feature selection:

a. Filter Methods

Filter methods select features based on statistical properties, independently of the model. These methods assess features according to their correlation with the target variable.

- **Correlation Coefficients**: Calculate the correlation between each feature and the target, removing features with low correlation.
- **Chi-Square Test**: For categorical data, the chi-square test evaluates whether there's a significant association between each feature and the target variable.

b. Wrapper Methods

Wrapper methods use iterative model-based evaluations to select features, considering the performance of subsets of features on a specific model. Techniques include:

- **Forward Selection**: Starts with no features and adds features one at a time, choosing those that improve model performance the most.

- **Backward Elimination**: Starts with all features and removes the least impactful features one at a time, observing the effect on performance.

c. Embedded Methods

Embedded methods perform feature selection within the training process of the model itself. Regularization techniques like Lasso and Ridge regression add a penalty to the model to reduce the importance of less impactful features.

- **Lasso (L1 Regularization)**: Adds a penalty equal to the absolute value of the feature coefficients, forcing some coefficients to zero, thus excluding irrelevant features.
- **Ridge (L2 Regularization)**: Adds a penalty equal to the square of the coefficients, reducing the influence of less important features without forcing them to zero.

d. Principal Component Analysis (PCA)

PCA is a dimensionality reduction technique that transforms features into a smaller set of components based on the variance in the data. PCA reduces complexity while retaining essential information.

- **Application**: PCA is useful in high-dimensional datasets where many features are correlated. By transforming features into principal components, PCA preserves variance and reduces redundancy.

e. Recursive Feature Elimination (RFE)

RFE is a recursive wrapper method that uses a model to rank features by importance and iteratively removes the least important features. It's a robust approach that can work with a variety of algorithms.

- **Application**: RFE is useful in datasets with many features where traditional filter methods may overlook complex relationships. It's often used with models like decision trees or support vector machines.

4. Reducing Dimensionality for Better Model Performance

High-dimensional data can be computationally expensive, complex, and prone to overfitting. Dimensionality reduction techniques help simplify the dataset while preserving essential information, leading to faster training and improved generalization.

a. Feature Scaling and Normalization

Scaling and normalizing data are essential steps when working with models sensitive to feature scales, such as K-nearest neighbors or SVM. Common methods include:

- **Standardization**: Scales features to have a mean of zero and a standard deviation of one, making them comparable.
- **Normalization**: Scales features to a range, typically between 0 and 1, reducing the impact of large feature values.

b. Selecting Principal Components with PCA

As discussed, PCA reduces dimensionality by converting features into a smaller set of principal components. PCA is valuable when dealing with correlated variables, as it combines them into uncorrelated components that retain most of the variance.

c. t-SNE for Visualization

Although t-SNE (t-distributed stochastic neighbor embedding) is primarily used for visualization, it reduces high-dimensional data into two or three dimensions, highlighting clusters and patterns. t-SNE is particularly helpful in visualizing the relationships in complex datasets.

Example of Dimensionality Reduction

Customer Churn Prediction in Telecommunications

A telecommunications company wants to predict customer churn using customer demographic and usage data, which includes dozens of features. By applying PCA, the company reduces the dataset to the principal components that explain most of the variance, streamlining the dataset without sacrificing valuable information. The resulting data improves model training time and accuracy, leading to a more effective churn prediction model.

5. Practical Tips for Effective Feature Engineering and Selection

To get the most out of feature engineering and selection, here are some best practices:

- **Experiment with Multiple Techniques**: Try different feature engineering methods (e.g., interaction terms, aggregations) and compare results to identify the most effective features.
- **Use Domain Knowledge**: Incorporate insights from the domain to create relevant features that align with business goals. For instance, using seasonality in retail data can improve predictions of sales cycles.

- **Avoid Data Leakage**: Ensure that features derived from future data are not included in the training set, as this can lead to artificially high accuracy.
- **Automate Feature Engineering with Tools**: Explore tools like FeatureTools or automated machine learning (AutoML) platforms, which assist in creating and testing features more efficiently.
- **Validate Results with Cross-Validation**: Use cross-validation to confirm that selected features generalize well across different parts of the dataset, ensuring robustness.

Conclusion

Effective feature engineering and selection are the cornerstones of building successful machine learning models. By crafting high-impact features, reducing dimensionality, and selecting the most relevant variables, analysts can significantly improve model accuracy, reduce complexity, and ensure the model's ability to generalize. Mastering these techniques enables data scientists and analysts to leverage raw data more effectively, uncover hidden insights, and deliver powerful, predictive models that drive business impact. As we continue, we'll delve deeper into advanced techniques for model tuning and evaluation, building on the foundation of strong feature engineering and selection.

Detailed Walk-Throughs of Feature Engineering Techniques Like Encoding, Scaling, and Extraction

Feature engineering is a transformative process in machine learning, turning raw data into valuable input for models. Techniques like encoding, scaling, and extraction allow analysts to prepare data so that machine learning algorithms can understand, learn, and make accurate predictions. This chapter provides detailed, step-by-step walk-throughs of these essential techniques, offering practical guidance on how to apply them for optimal machine learning success.

1. Encoding Categorical Variables: Converting Categories to Numeric Values

Machine learning models require numerical input, so categorical data must be converted into numerical format. Encoding categorical variables allows models to capture patterns within categories and relationships among them.

Encoding Techniques

- **One-Hot Encoding**: One-hot encoding converts each category into a separate binary column (0 or 1), where each column represents the presence or absence of a category.
  - ○ **When to Use**: One-hot encoding is effective for nominal (unordered) categories, such as "city," "color," or "product type."
  - ○ **Example**: Suppose we have a "Color" column with categories "Red," "Green," and "Blue." One-hot encoding would create three binary columns—Color_Red, Color_Green, and

Color_Blue—where each entry has a 1 in the column representing its color.

- **Label Encoding**: Label encoding assigns each category a unique integer, making it easy to interpret, but it can impose an unintended ordinal relationship.
  - **When to Use**: Use label encoding for ordinal categories where there is an inherent order, like "low," "medium," and "high."
  - **Example**: For an "Education" level column with values "High School," "Bachelor's," and "Master's," label encoding could map these values to 1, 2, and 3, respectively.
- **Target Encoding**: This technique replaces categories with the mean target variable value within each category, often used for high-cardinality categorical features.
  - **When to Use**: Target encoding is useful for reducing dimensionality in categorical data with many levels, such as "zipcode."
  - **Example**: For a "Region" feature predicting sales, target encoding might replace each region with its average sales.

Best Practices for Encoding

- **Avoid High Cardinality**: When possible, group categories with many unique values into broader categories to avoid excessive columns in one-hot encoding.

- **Beware of Data Leakage**: When using target encoding, ensure that you apply encoding on training data only, and not on test data, to prevent data leakage.

2. Scaling and Normalization: Standardizing Data Ranges

Scaling and normalization standardize feature values, making them comparable. These techniques are essential when working with algorithms that are sensitive to feature magnitudes, such as K-nearest neighbors (KNN) and support vector machines (SVM).

Scaling Techniques

- **Standardization (Z-score Normalization)**: Standardization transforms data to have a mean of zero and a standard deviation of one. It centers the data, making all features comparable without losing the original data distribution.
  - **When to Use**: Standardization is effective when features have different units or ranges, such as height (inches) and weight (pounds).
  - **Example**: For a dataset with income and age, standardizing both features ensures they are on the same scale, preventing income from disproportionately affecting the model.
- **Min-Max Normalization**: This method rescales data to a specified range, typically between 0 and 1. Min-max normalization is particularly helpful in cases where all values must be positive.

- o **When to Use**: Use min-max scaling for algorithms where the range of features impacts performance, such as neural networks.
  - o **Example**: For a dataset of house prices ranging from \$100,000 to \$1,000,000, min-max normalization would scale each price between 0 and 1, preserving relative distances.
- **Robust Scaling**: Robust scaling scales data based on the interquartile range (IQR), reducing the influence of outliers. It's effective when datasets contain extreme values.
  - o **When to Use**: Apply robust scaling when you suspect the presence of outliers that could skew the data.
  - o **Example**: In income data where a few extreme values exist, robust scaling limits the effect of these outliers on the overall data distribution.

Practical Tips for Scaling
- **Apply Scaling After Train-Test Split**: Always split the dataset into training and testing sets before scaling to avoid data leakage.
- **Choose the Appropriate Scaling Method**: Select the scaling method based on the characteristics of the dataset and the algorithm's sensitivity to scale.

3. Feature Extraction: Reducing Complexity While Retaining Information

Feature extraction techniques help condense information from multiple features into a smaller set, capturing essential information while simplifying the dataset. This approach is particularly useful for high-dimensional datasets where many features are redundant.

Feature Extraction Techniques

- **Principal Component Analysis (PCA)**: PCA reduces dimensionality by transforming features into a smaller set of uncorrelated components, each representing a combination of the original features that capture maximum variance.
  - **When to Use**: PCA is ideal for high-dimensional data where features are correlated, such as gene expression or image data.
  - **Example**: In a customer dataset with dozens of demographic and behavioral features, PCA might reduce the data to a few principal components, making analysis more manageable while retaining critical information.
- **t-Distributed Stochastic Neighbor Embedding (t-SNE)**: Primarily used for data visualization, t-SNE maps high-dimensional data to two or three dimensions, preserving local relationships to highlight clusters.
  - **When to Use**: t-SNE is useful for visualizing complex patterns, such as clusters in text or image data.
  - **Example**: For visualizing customer segments, t-SNE can reduce hundreds of features into a two-dimensional map, allowing analysts to identify clusters based on customer behaviors.

- **Feature Hashing**: Feature hashing converts high-cardinality categorical data into a fixed-size numeric representation, often used in text data and situations where dimensionality reduction is needed.
  - ○ **When to Use**: Apply feature hashing for large categorical data (e.g., product IDs or URLs) where traditional encoding methods would lead to high dimensionality.
  - ○ **Example**: For a large text dataset with thousands of unique words, feature hashing reduces the number of dimensions, making the model training process faster.
- **Text Vectorization (TF-IDF)**: Term Frequency-Inverse Document Frequency (TF-IDF) is a feature extraction method for text data, assigning weights to words based on their frequency and uniqueness in a document.
  - ○ **When to Use**: Use TF-IDF for text classification, sentiment analysis, or any task involving textual data.
  - ○ **Example**: In sentiment analysis, TF-IDF transforms a review's words into numerical values, highlighting unique words while downplaying common ones, helping the model focus on meaningful terms.

Practical Tips for Feature Extraction
- **Combine with Feature Selection**: After feature extraction, use selection techniques to identify which extracted features are most predictive.

- **Interpret Principal Components Carefully**: PCA components are combinations of original features, which may make them harder to interpret. Use feature loadings to understand the contribution of each feature.
- **Optimize for Task Requirements**: Choose the extraction method based on the dataset's characteristics and the specific analysis goals (e.g., TF-IDF for text, PCA for high-dimensional data).

4. Creating Aggregation Features: Summarizing Data at Different Levels

Aggregation involves creating summary features based on groups within the data, providing insights across different levels of granularity. Aggregation features can capture underlying patterns that are not visible in raw data.

Types of Aggregation Features

- **Temporal Aggregates**: Summarize data over specific time periods, such as weekly averages, monthly totals, or year-to-date sums.
  - **Example**: In a sales dataset, aggregating monthly sales per store helps detect seasonal patterns and store performance.
- **Group-Level Aggregates**: Calculate statistics based on groups, such as averages, counts, or sums for each customer, product, or region.
  - **Example**: In customer data, calculating the average purchase value per customer or the total visits per customer reveals patterns in spending behavior.

90

- **Rolling Aggregates**: Compute moving averages or rolling sums over a fixed window, allowing for trend analysis.
  - Example: In financial data, a 7-day moving average of stock prices smooths out daily fluctuations, highlighting broader trends.

Practical Tips for Aggregation Features

- **Select Appropriate Time Windows**: Choose aggregation windows that reflect natural business cycles (e.g., weekly, monthly) to capture meaningful trends.
- **Avoid Data Leakage**: When creating time-based aggregates, ensure that future data is not included in calculations to prevent data leakage.
- **Experiment with Different Aggregations**: Test various types of aggregations to identify which ones enhance model performance the most.

5. Practical Example: End-to-End Feature Engineering Process

Scenario: Predicting Customer Churn for a Subscription Service

- **Encoding**: Convert the categorical "Subscription Type" column into one-hot encoding, creating binary columns for each subscription level.
- **Scaling**: Standardize numerical features like "Monthly Spend" and "Customer Age" to ensure they're on the same scale.

- **Feature Extraction**: Use PCA on behavioral data (e.g., weekly usage statistics) to reduce dimensions and focus on core usage patterns.
- **Aggregation**: Create temporal aggregates for "Total Usage Last 3 Months" and "Average Weekly Visits," capturing recent engagement trends.
- **Final Model Preparation**: Select the most predictive features, ensuring only the most impactful data remains for model training.

This end-to-end feature engineering process transforms raw customer data into a structured dataset ready for modeling, maximizing predictive power while reducing complexity.

Conclusion

Feature engineering and selection are integral to the success of any machine learning model. By understanding and applying techniques like encoding, scaling, and extraction, data professionals can optimize their datasets, enhancing both model performance and interpretability. Mastery of these techniques allows analysts to transform raw data into meaningful, actionable features that drive machine learning success. As we progress, these engineered features will serve as the foundation for building and evaluating robust models that deliver business value.

Practical Examples of Feature Selection Methods That Improve Model Accuracy and Efficiency

Feature selection is the process of identifying the most relevant features from a dataset to enhance model accuracy, reduce computational complexity, and improve interpretability. Selecting the right features eliminates noise, prevents overfitting, and often results in faster and more accurate models. This chapter provides practical examples of commonly used feature selection methods, demonstrating how each approach contributes to building better-performing machine learning models.

1. Filter Methods: Ranking Features Based on Statistical Properties

Filter methods evaluate each feature independently of the model, ranking features based on statistical metrics like correlation or mutual information. These techniques are often the first step in feature selection, as they are fast and effective for high-dimensional datasets.

Example: Using Correlation Coefficient for Feature Selection in House Price Prediction

In a house price prediction model, we have numerous features like square footage, number of rooms, age, location, and proximity to schools. To identify the most relevant features, we calculate the correlation of each feature with the target variable (house price).

- **Process**: Calculate the Pearson correlation coefficient between each feature and house price. Features with high positive or negative correlations (e.g., square footage, location) are likely to have more predictive power.

- **Outcome**: By selecting features with a correlation coefficient above a chosen threshold (e.g., 0.3 or -0.3), we retain features that are highly relevant while discarding weakly correlated features.

- **Impact**: Reducing the feature set to only those with strong correlations improves model interpretability and accuracy, as the model focuses on features that meaningfully affect house prices.

Best Practices for Filter Methods

- **Apply Before Model Training**: Use filter methods as an initial step to remove low-value features and reduce dimensionality quickly.
- **Consider Multicollinearity**: Avoid including highly correlated features simultaneously, as they add redundancy. In this example, if square footage and number of rooms are highly correlated, choose one to prevent multicollinearity.

2. Wrapper Methods: Iteratively Selecting Features Using Model Performance

Wrapper methods assess the predictive power of feature subsets by training the model multiple times. This approach can provide higher accuracy than filter methods, although it can be computationally intensive.

Example: Forward Selection in Customer Churn Prediction

For a customer churn prediction model, we start with a blank slate and iteratively add features based on their ability to improve model performance.

- **Process**: Begin with no features, add one feature at a time, and evaluate model performance (e.g., using accuracy or AUC score). Retain features that improve model performance and continue adding until there's no further improvement.

- **Outcome**: Forward selection might identify features such as "monthly usage," "contract type," and "customer tenure" as highly predictive, while excluding features that don't add value (e.g., minor demographic details).
- **Impact**: Focusing only on the features that drive predictive power increases model accuracy while reducing the risk of overfitting. This streamlined feature set also leads to faster training and prediction times.

Best Practices for Wrapper Methods

- **Be Aware of Computational Costs**: Wrapper methods require multiple model runs, so use with smaller datasets or fewer features, or apply after an initial filter.
- **Monitor Model Overfitting**: Wrapper methods can lead to overfitting if not properly cross-validated, especially on small datasets.

3. Embedded Methods: Selecting Features During Model Training

Embedded methods perform feature selection within the training process, allowing the model to decide which features are most predictive. These techniques integrate regularization, penalizing less impactful features, and can improve both accuracy and efficiency.

Example: Lasso (L1 Regularization) in Predicting Loan Default

In predicting loan default, a financial institution uses numerous features, such as income, credit score, employment history, and existing debt. By applying Lasso regression, we can automatically select impactful features while penalizing less important ones.

- **Process**: Train the model with Lasso regression, which adds an L1 penalty to the objective function, pushing the coefficients of less important features to zero.
- **Outcome**: Features with non-zero coefficients (e.g., income, credit score) are retained, while redundant features (e.g., zip code, minor loan details) are eliminated.
- **Impact**: This approach improves model interpretability by highlighting the most important features and reduces the risk of overfitting, as irrelevant features are effectively ignored.

Best Practices for Embedded Methods

- **Choose the Right Regularization Method**: Use L1 regularization (Lasso) for sparse data or when you expect only a few features to be highly predictive.
- **Optimize Regularization Parameter**: Adjust the regularization strength (lambda) to balance feature elimination with model accuracy.

4. Principal Component Analysis (PCA): Reducing Dimensionality While Preserving Variance

PCA is a powerful dimensionality reduction technique that combines features into principal components based on variance, reducing complexity while retaining essential information. PCA is particularly effective for high-dimensional data where features are highly correlated.

Example: Dimensionality Reduction in Image Recognition
In an image recognition dataset with thousands of pixel features, training a model on every pixel is computationally prohibitive. PCA reduces the dataset to a manageable number of components.

- **Process**: Apply PCA to transform the pixel features into principal components, each representing a portion of the data variance. Select the top components that explain 95% of the variance.
- **Outcome**: The original dataset with thousands of features is reduced to a smaller set of components (e.g., the top 50 components), preserving most of the information.
- **Impact**: PCA reduces the training time and memory usage, while retaining the predictive power needed for accurate image recognition. This approach also helps prevent overfitting by focusing on core patterns rather than noise.

Best Practices for PCA

- **Standardize Features Before Applying PCA**: Ensure features are standardized to have a mean of zero and a standard deviation of one for consistent component scaling.
- **Select the Number of Components Based on Variance**: Choose components that capture most of the variance (e.g., 95%), balancing dimensionality reduction with information retention.

5. Recursive Feature Elimination (RFE): Iterative Removal Based on Model Performance

RFE is an iterative wrapper method that ranks features by importance and removes the least important ones in each iteration until reaching a specified number of features. RFE works well with algorithms that can assign feature importance, like decision trees or support vector machines.

Example: Feature Selection in Sentiment Analysis

In a sentiment analysis model using thousands of text features (words), many terms may add little value. RFE helps identify the most impactful words while reducing noise.

- **Process**: Use a model (e.g., SVM or logistic regression) to rank features by importance, remove the least impactful features iteratively, and retain the top features based on accuracy.
- **Outcome**: RFE identifies the most relevant words, such as "excellent" and "poor," while removing common or less meaningful words like "the" or "and."
- **Impact**: The resulting feature set improves model accuracy by focusing on words that contribute to sentiment prediction, reducing dimensionality and making the model faster and more interpretable.

Best Practices for RFE

- **Use with Feature Importance-Estimating Models**: Apply RFE with models that calculate feature importance, such as decision trees, SVM, or linear models.

- **Cross-Validate Results**: Validate RFE-selected features across multiple folds to ensure robustness and avoid overfitting.

6. Mutual Information: Quantifying the Predictive Power of Categorical Features

Mutual information measures the dependency between features and the target variable, capturing both linear and non-linear relationships. It is particularly useful for feature selection in classification tasks with categorical data.

Example: Predicting Product Recommendations Based on User Behavior

In a product recommendation system, we analyze categorical features such as user device type, country, and past product interactions. Mutual information quantifies the importance of each feature in predicting the likelihood of a product purchase.

- **Process**: Calculate mutual information for each categorical feature relative to the target variable, selecting features with the highest scores.
- **Outcome**: Retain features like "past purchases" and "device type" that have high predictive power, while discarding features with low mutual information.
- **Impact**: By focusing on features with high mutual information, the recommendation system makes more accurate predictions, increasing customer engagement and conversion rates.

Best Practices for Mutual Information

- **Handle Continuous Variables Separately**: Mutual information is most effective with categorical features, so consider using other methods for continuous variables.

- **Combine with Other Methods**: Use mutual information alongside other feature selection techniques for a comprehensive approach.

Conclusion

Feature selection methods like filter methods, wrapper methods, embedded techniques, PCA, RFE, and mutual information are invaluable tools for improving model accuracy and efficiency. Each technique offers unique benefits depending on the dataset and task, and by understanding when and how to apply each method, data scientists can streamline feature sets to build faster, more interpretable, and more accurate machine learning models. This careful selection of features forms a solid foundation for model training, enabling machine learning models to achieve optimal performance and create real business value. As we continue, we'll explore advanced methods for model tuning and validation, building on this foundation of effective feature engineering and selection.

Chapter 6: Evaluating and Optimizing Models: Beyond the Basics

Advanced Techniques for Evaluating Model Performance, Including ROC-AUC, Precision-Recall, and More

Model evaluation is a critical step in machine learning, determining whether a model is reliable and ready for deployment. Beyond standard accuracy, advanced evaluation techniques like ROC-AUC, precision-recall, and F1-score provide deeper insights into model performance, especially when dealing with imbalanced classes or complex classification tasks. This chapter explores these advanced metrics and techniques to help analysts evaluate and optimize models effectively.

1. Importance of Choosing the Right Evaluation Metric

Selecting the right evaluation metric depends on the nature of the problem, the data distribution, and the business objective. While accuracy is often used as a baseline metric, it can be misleading in scenarios like imbalanced classification, where correctly identifying the minority class is critical.

Considerations for Selecting Evaluation Metrics

- **Imbalanced Datasets**: When classes are imbalanced, metrics like precision, recall, and F1-score become more important than accuracy.
- **Prediction Objective**: For tasks where false positives and false negatives carry different costs, metrics like precision, recall, and ROC-AUC are critical.

- **Application Context**: In fields like healthcare and finance, where the cost of misclassification is high, careful metric selection is essential for risk mitigation.

2. Confusion Matrix: The Foundation of Classification Metrics

The confusion matrix is a table that summarizes model predictions by counting true positives (TP), true negatives (TN), false positives (FP), and false negatives (FN). From this matrix, other metrics are derived.

Example: Fraud Detection in Banking

In a fraud detection model, each prediction is categorized into one of four classes:

- **True Positive (TP)**: Correctly predicted fraudulent transaction.
- **True Negative (TN)**: Correctly predicted non-fraudulent transaction.
- **False Positive (FP)**: Incorrectly predicted fraudulent transaction (non-fraud flagged as fraud).
- **False Negative (FN)**: Incorrectly predicted non-fraudulent transaction (fraud not detected).

This breakdown allows for calculating metrics such as accuracy, precision, recall, and F1-score.

3. Precision and Recall: Balancing False Positives and False Negatives

Precision and recall are particularly useful for imbalanced classification tasks where the cost of false positives or false negatives varies.

- **Precision**: Precision, or positive predictive value, measures the proportion of true positives out of all positive predictions. A high precision indicates fewer false positives.
  - ○ **Formula**: Precision = TP / (TP + FP)
  - ○ **Example**: In fraud detection, high precision means that most transactions flagged as fraudulent are indeed fraud, reducing unnecessary investigations.
- **Recall**: Recall, or sensitivity, measures the proportion of true positives out of all actual positives. High recall means fewer false negatives.
  - ○ **Formula**: Recall = TP / (TP + FN)
  - ○ **Example**: In medical diagnosis, high recall ensures that most actual cases (e.g., disease presence) are correctly identified, minimizing missed cases.

F1-Score: Balancing Precision and Recall

The F1-score is the harmonic mean of precision and recall, providing a single metric to balance both. It is useful when both false positives and false negatives are costly.

- **Formula**: F1 = 2 * (Precision * Recall) / (Precision + Recall)
- **Example**: In email spam detection, a high F1-score indicates a good balance between identifying spam accurately and minimizing false positives (non-spam marked as spam).

Choosing Between Precision, Recall, and F1-Score

- Use **precision** when false positives carry a higher cost.
- Use **recall** when false negatives carry a higher cost.
- Use **F1-score** when both false positives and false negatives have similar costs.

4. ROC-AUC: Evaluating Classifier Performance Across Thresholds

The Receiver Operating Characteristic (ROC) curve plots the true positive rate (sensitivity) against the false positive rate (1-specificity) at various threshold levels. The Area Under the Curve (AUC) summarizes the ROC curve into a single value, indicating how well the model separates classes.

- **Interpreting ROC-AUC**: An AUC score of 0.5 indicates random performance, while 1.0 represents a perfect classifier. Higher AUC values indicate better model performance.
- **Example**: In customer churn prediction, ROC-AUC helps visualize how well the model discriminates between churners and non-churners, guiding decisions on the probability threshold for labeling churners.

Using ROC-AUC in Imbalanced Data

- ROC-AUC is not always ideal for highly imbalanced datasets, as it considers both true and false positives equally. In such cases, precision-recall curves provide more insight.

5. Precision-Recall Curve: Performance with Imbalanced Classes

The precision-recall (PR) curve plots precision against recall at different threshold settings, providing a clearer picture of model performance with imbalanced classes. The area under the PR curve (PR-AUC) summarizes the model's ability to balance precision and recall.

- **Interpreting the Precision-Recall Curve**: A high area under the PR curve indicates effective performance, particularly in detecting the minority class.
- **Example**: In fraud detection, the PR curve can show how the model balances identifying actual fraud cases while avoiding false positives. PR-AUC is more informative than ROC-AUC in this scenario.

When to Use Precision-Recall Curves

- Use PR curves in cases where true negatives are abundant and less relevant (e.g., fraud detection, disease diagnosis).
- PR curves provide better insight into model performance on the minority class, which is often the focus in imbalanced datasets.

6. Advanced Metrics for Regression Models

While classification metrics focus on true/false predictions, regression models require different evaluation metrics to assess prediction accuracy.

Common Regression Metrics

- **Mean Absolute Error (MAE)**: Measures the average magnitude of prediction errors, providing an intuitive interpretation of model accuracy.
  - **Formula**: MAE = $(1/n) * \Sigma$ |Actual - Predicted|

- o **Example**: In forecasting housing prices, MAE gives an average dollar deviation from the true price.
- **Mean Squared Error (MSE) and Root Mean Squared Error (RMSE)**: MSE emphasizes larger errors by squaring them, while RMSE provides results in the same units as the target variable.
  - o **Formula**: MSE = $(1/n) * \Sigma$ (Actual - Predicted)^2, RMSE = $\sqrt{MSE}$
  - o **Example**: RMSE is useful in time-series forecasting, where small prediction errors are acceptable but large errors need emphasis.
- **R-squared (R^2)**: Measures the proportion of variance explained by the model. Higher values indicate a better fit.
  - o **Formula**: R^2 = 1 - (SS_residual / SS_total)
  - o **Example**: In advertising spend vs. sales forecasting, a high R^2 value shows that advertising spend explains a large portion of sales variation.

Choosing Regression Metrics

- Use **MAE** when you want a direct interpretation of error magnitude.
- Use **MSE** or **RMSE** to penalize larger errors.
- Use **R^2** to understand how well the model explains the variance in the data.

7. Cross-Validation for Robust Model Evaluation

Cross-validation splits the dataset into multiple subsets, training and testing the model on each subset to ensure robustness. Common techniques include:

- **K-Fold Cross-Validation**: Divides the data into k subsets, trains on k-1 subsets, and tests on the remaining one. This process repeats k times, providing a robust performance estimate.
  - o **Example**: In image recognition, 10-fold cross-validation helps ensure model accuracy without overfitting to a single subset of data.
- **Leave-One-Out Cross-Validation (LOOCV)**: Each data point is used once as a test set while the rest form the training set. LOOCV is ideal for small datasets but can be computationally expensive.
  - o **Example**: In medical datasets with limited samples, LOOCV maximizes the use of all available data.

Benefits of Cross-Validation

- Reduces the likelihood of overfitting and underfitting by validating performance across multiple data subsets.
- Provides a more accurate measure of model performance on unseen data.

8. Hyperparameter Tuning to Optimize Model Performance

Hyperparameter tuning optimizes model performance by selecting the best set of parameters for the algorithm. Techniques include:

- **Grid Search**: Tests all combinations of a predefined parameter grid to identify the best settings.
- **Random Search**: Randomly samples parameters from the grid, making it faster than grid search for large parameter spaces.
- **Bayesian Optimization**: Uses probabilistic models to estimate the best parameters, iteratively refining search space based on previous results.

Example: Tuning Hyperparameters in a Random Forest Model

In a random forest model for predicting loan defaults, hyperparameters like the number of trees, maximum depth, and minimum samples per leaf affect performance. Using grid search, we test combinations of these parameters to find the set that yields the highest cross-validation accuracy.

Tips for Effective Hyperparameter Tuning

- Use cross-validation during tuning to prevent overfitting.
- Limit grid size or use random search to reduce computation time on large datasets.

Conclusion

Evaluating and optimizing models requires more than just standard accuracy metrics. Advanced techniques like ROC-AUC, precision-recall curves, F1-score, and cross-validation provide a comprehensive view of model performance, allowing data scientists to choose the best metrics for their problem. Hyperparameter tuning further refines model parameters, optimizing for accuracy and efficiency. By applying these advanced techniques, machine learning practitioners can develop robust, high-performing models that meet specific business objectives and deliver meaningful insights. Moving forward, these evaluation and optimization methods will play a crucial role in ensuring models are ready for deployment and real-world application.

Guide to Hyperparameter Tuning, Cross-Validation, and Ensemble Methods for Boosting Performance

In machine learning, building an accurate model is only the beginning. To achieve the best performance, it's essential to refine and optimize the model through techniques like hyperparameter tuning, cross-validation, and ensemble methods. These techniques help extract maximum predictive power from the model, ensuring it generalizes well to new data. This chapter covers practical strategies for fine-tuning hyperparameters, validating models effectively, and using ensemble methods to boost performance.

1. Hyperparameter Tuning: Fine-Tuning Model Parameters for Optimal Performance

Hyperparameters are model parameters set before training that significantly influence performance. Unlike parameters learned from data (like weights in neural networks), hyperparameters control the training process itself, such as learning rate, maximum depth of trees, or regularization strength.

Hyperparameter Tuning Methods

- **Grid Search**: Grid search exhaustively tests all possible combinations within a specified set of hyperparameter values.
    - Example: In a support vector machine (SVM), grid search might test different values for the kernel type, regularization parameter (C), and gamma. Grid search identifies the combination that yields the best model performance on the validation set.
    - Pros: Comprehensive and ensures that every combination is tested.
    - Cons: Computationally expensive, especially with large parameter grids.
- **Random Search**: Rather than testing all combinations, random search selects random hyperparameter combinations from a predefined range.
    - Example: For a random forest model, random search may randomly select values for the number of trees and maximum depth to find an effective combination.
    - Pros: Faster than grid search, especially when the hyperparameter space is large.
    - Cons: May miss the optimal combination but still finds reasonably good results.
- **Bayesian Optimization**: Uses probabilistic models to predict the best parameters based on previous results, refining the search over iterations.

- Example: In a gradient boosting model, Bayesian optimization might adjust learning rate, number of estimators, and maximum depth iteratively to maximize accuracy.
- Pros: Efficient and smart search, focusing on promising regions of the hyperparameter space.
- Cons: More complex to implement but often more computationally efficient than grid search.

Best Practices for Hyperparameter Tuning

- **Start with Random or Grid Search**: Use these methods to get a sense of the hyperparameter space before refining with Bayesian optimization.
- **Use Cross-Validation**: Perform hyperparameter tuning with cross-validation to ensure generalizability and avoid overfitting.
- **Track Results**: Use tools like logging frameworks or experiment tracking to monitor combinations and their outcomes for future reference.

2. Cross-Validation: Ensuring Robust Model Performance

Cross-validation divides the dataset into multiple subsets, iterating the model training and evaluation process to assess its stability and generalizability. Cross-validation provides a more accurate measure of model performance than a single train-test split, reducing the risk of overfitting or underfitting.

Common Cross-Validation Techniques

- **K-Fold Cross-Validation**: The dataset is divided into k subsets, and the model is trained on k-1 subsets while the remaining subset serves as the validation set. This process repeats k times, with each subset used once as the validation set.

- o **Example**: In a 5-fold cross-validation, the dataset is split into 5 subsets, and the model is trained and evaluated five times. The average performance across folds provides a robust estimate.
- o **Pros**: Effective and suitable for most datasets.
- o **Cons**: Can be computationally intensive with larger datasets or high k values.
- **Stratified K-Fold**: Ensures each fold has the same class distribution as the entire dataset, which is especially useful for imbalanced datasets.
  - o **Example**: In a binary classification task with 10% positives and 90% negatives, stratified K-fold maintains this ratio within each fold.
  - o **Pros**: Maintains class balance, improving reliability for imbalanced datasets.
  - o **Cons**: Similar computational requirements to standard K-fold.
- **Leave-One-Out Cross-Validation (LOOCV)**: Uses each individual data point as a validation set while training on the remaining points, repeating for every data point.
  - o **Example**: For a dataset with 100 samples, the model trains 99 samples each time and tests on the 1 remaining sample, repeating this process 100 times.

- o **Pros**: Useful for small datasets, maximizes training data use.
- o **Cons**: Computationally expensive, not practical for large datasets.

Best Practices for Cross-Validation

- **Choose the Right k-Value**: A higher k (e.g., 10) provides a more reliable performance estimate but increases computational cost. Select a balance based on dataset size.
- **Use Stratified K-Fold for Classification**: This ensures balanced class representation within each fold, especially helpful in imbalanced datasets.
- **Track Cross-Validation Scores**: Calculate and monitor the mean and standard deviation of cross-validation scores to assess model consistency.

3. Ensemble Methods: Combining Models for Enhanced Performance

Ensemble methods improve model accuracy and robustness by combining the predictions of multiple models. This approach reduces variance and bias, often resulting in better overall performance than individual models.

Popular Ensemble Techniques

- **Bagging (Bootstrap Aggregating)**: Trains multiple models on different subsets of the data and aggregates their predictions. Random forests, a popular bagging method, use multiple decision trees to increase stability and accuracy.

- Example: In a random forest for credit scoring, each tree may assess customer risk differently, and the forest's final prediction averages these results.
- Pros: Reduces overfitting and variance, ideal for high-variance models like decision trees.
- Cons: Requires more computational power due to multiple model training.
- **Boosting**: Sequentially trains models, with each model correcting errors from the previous one. Common algorithms include AdaBoost, Gradient Boosting, and XGBoost.
  - Example: In predicting customer churn, boosting models focus on difficult-to-predict samples, gradually improving performance.
  - Pros: High accuracy, especially effective for weak learners.
  - Cons: Prone to overfitting if not carefully tuned, computationally intensive.
- **Stacking**: Combines different model types by training a "meta-model" on the predictions of base models. The meta-model learns how to best combine the base models' predictions for optimal results.
  - Example: A stacking ensemble for housing price prediction might combine the outputs of a decision tree, a linear regression, and a neural network, using a meta-model to blend these predictions.

- Pros: Flexible and leverages strengths of diverse models.
- Cons: Complex to implement and requires careful tuning of base and meta-models.

Practical Example: Using XGBoost for Boosting Performance

In a loan default prediction model, XGBoost is used due to its flexibility and high accuracy. Hyperparameters like learning rate, max depth, and number of estimators are tuned using cross-validation to balance accuracy and prevent overfitting.

- **Step 1**: Perform grid search to find the optimal combination of learning rate and max depth.
- **Step 2**: Apply 5-fold cross-validation to validate performance.
- **Step 3**: Monitor feature importance scores in XGBoost, using only the most impactful features for final tuning.
- **Impact**: The tuned XGBoost model achieves higher precision and recall than single models, making it reliable for predicting defaults with minimal false positives and negatives.

Best Practices for Ensemble Methods

- **Optimize Individual Models**: Tune each base model individually before combining them in an ensemble.
- **Use Voting for Simplicity**: In classification, simple voting (majority for classification, average for regression) is effective when combining similar models.

- **Regularize Boosting Models**: Apply regularization techniques in boosting (e.g., shrinkage in gradient boosting) to avoid overfitting.

4. Practical Steps for Implementing a Comprehensive Evaluation and Optimization Workflow

To ensure robust model performance, a structured workflow is key. This workflow combines hyperparameter tuning, cross-validation, and ensemble methods for systematic model optimization.

Step-by-Step Workflow

1. **Initial Model Training**: Start with a simple model to establish a baseline for performance.
2. **Initial Hyperparameter Tuning**: Use grid search or random search to narrow down a reasonable hyperparameter range.
3. **Cross-Validation**: Validate model stability and reliability using K-fold cross-validation.
4. **Refine Hyperparameters with Bayesian Optimization**: Apply Bayesian optimization to fine-tune hyperparameters within the best-performing range.
5. **Apply Ensemble Methods**: Experiment with bagging (e.g., random forest), boosting (e.g., XGBoost), or stacking for further improvements.
6. **Evaluate with Advanced Metrics**: Use ROC-AUC, precision-recall curves, or F1-score for final evaluation, ensuring performance meets business needs.

Case Study Example: Fraud Detection Model in Banking

In a fraud detection model:

- **Step 1**: Random search is used to tune initial parameters for a random forest model.
- **Step 2**: 10-fold cross-validation assesses stability, ensuring performance across folds.
- **Step 3**: Bayesian optimization further tunes max depth and minimum sample splits.
- **Step 4**: A stacking ensemble combines the tuned random forest, logistic regression, and XGBoost for optimal performance.
- **Step 5**: The model is evaluated with ROC-AUC and PR curves, confirming high precision and recall in fraud detection.

Outcome: This structured process results in a robust, accurate fraud detection model that generalizes well, minimizes false positives, and meets regulatory standards.

Conclusion

Advanced techniques like hyperparameter tuning, cross-validation, and ensemble methods are essential for developing high-performing machine learning models. By following a structured workflow that includes these techniques, data scientists can build models that maximize accuracy, minimize overfitting, and generalize well to new data. Through systematic optimization, these models provide reliable predictions and insights, allowing businesses to make informed, data-driven decisions with confidence. As we proceed, these evaluation and optimization strategies will prove invaluable in preparing models for deployment and real-world impact.

Introducing Model Interpretability for Transparency in Decision-Making

As machine learning models play an increasingly significant role in critical decision-making processes across industries, understanding and explaining model behavior has become essential. Model interpretability enhances transparency, helping stakeholders understand how predictions are made and ensuring that models align with ethical standards, regulatory requirements, and organizational goals. This chapter introduces key interpretability techniques that make models more transparent, enabling data scientists to balance predictive power with the need for trustworthy, explainable decisions.

1. Importance of Model Interpretability in Machine Learning

Interpretability is vital for ensuring that models are not only accurate but also understandable and actionable. Transparent models help build trust among stakeholders and allow organizations to validate model fairness, avoid biases, and ensure that model predictions are in line with domain knowledge.

Why Interpretability Matters

- **Trust and Transparency**: Interpretable models help stakeholders understand and trust predictions, especially when models influence high-stakes decisions (e.g., medical diagnoses, financial credit approvals).
- **Bias and Fairness Detection**: Interpretable models enable analysts to detect and mitigate bias, ensuring

that model outcomes are fair across demographic groups.

- **Compliance with Regulations**: In highly regulated fields, such as finance and healthcare, organizations must meet transparency standards to comply with data protection and fairness laws.

Challenges in Interpretability

- **Complexity vs. Simplicity**: Highly accurate models like deep neural networks and ensemble methods are often complex, making them harder to interpret than simpler models like linear regression.
- **Need for Explanations**: Stakeholders require explanations that are both technically accurate and accessible, balancing depth with clarity.

2. Global vs. Local Interpretability: Understanding the Scope of Explanation

Model interpretability can be divided into two types: global interpretability, which explains the overall model behavior, and local interpretability, which focuses on individual predictions. Both are essential for providing a comprehensive view of model decisions.

- **Global Interpretability**: Provides insights into how the model generally works, such as which features are most influential across all predictions.
  - **Example**: In a customer churn prediction model, global interpretability might reveal that "contract length" and "monthly charges" are the most important factors for predicting churn.

- **Local Interpretability**: Focuses on explaining the decision-making process for a specific prediction, highlighting the contributions of each feature in that instance.
  - o **Example**: In a healthcare model predicting disease risk, local interpretability explains why a specific patient is at high risk, detailing the influence of factors like age, blood pressure, and family history.

Choosing Between Global and Local Interpretability

- Use **global interpretability** for model insights, feature importance, and overall understanding.
- Use **local interpretability** to understand individual cases, particularly in applications requiring specific justifications (e.g., explaining why a loan application was rejected).

3. Feature Importance: Identifying Key Drivers of Model Predictions

Feature importance quantifies the contribution of each feature to the model's overall predictions, providing insights into the most influential factors driving model behavior.

Techniques for Measuring Feature Importance

- **Tree-Based Feature Importance**: Tree-based models, like random forests and gradient boosting, calculate feature importance by measuring the reduction in impurity each feature contributes across splits.
  - o **Example**: In a random forest for loan default prediction, "income level" may have the highest

importance score, indicating it's a key factor in predicting defaults.

- **Permutation Importance**: This technique measures the change in model performance when a feature's values are randomly shuffled. A significant drop in performance indicates that the feature is important.
  - ○ **Example**: If shuffling "monthly spending" in a customer segmentation model significantly decreases accuracy, it suggests that this feature is critical for segmentation.

Best Practices for Feature Importance

- **Use Permutation for Consistency**: Since permutation importance is model-agnostic, it's helpful when feature importances from tree-based models differ from reality.
- **Compare Across Models**: Evaluate feature importance across multiple models to verify which features consistently influence predictions.

4. SHAP (SHapley Additive exPlanations): Explaining Individual Predictions

SHAP values provide a unified approach to interpret individual predictions across various models, inspired by Shapley values from cooperative game theory. SHAP quantifies the contribution of each feature to the prediction for a specific instance, offering both local and global interpretability.

How SHAP Works

- **Global Interpretability**: SHAP generates average feature importance values, revealing which features have the largest impact across predictions.

- Example: In a model predicting customer loyalty, SHAP can show that "customer tenure" has the largest average impact on loyalty scores across the dataset.
- **Local Interpretability**: SHAP assigns values to each feature for a specific prediction, showing how each feature influences the outcome.
  - Example: For a customer predicted to churn, SHAP might show that "high monthly charges" and "lack of contract renewal" have the highest positive SHAP values, driving the prediction.

Advantages of SHAP
- **Model-Agnostic**: SHAP can be used with any model, making it versatile for explaining predictions across diverse model types.
- **Consistent Interpretations**: SHAP values are based on fair distribution principles, ensuring that feature contributions add up to the model's prediction.

Best Practices for Using SHAP
- **Visualize SHAP Values**: Use SHAP summary plots to visualize feature importance globally, and waterfall plots for local interpretability of individual predictions.
- **Combine with Feature Importance**: Use SHAP in conjunction with traditional feature importance to validate insights and deepen understanding.

5. LIME (Local Interpretable Model-agnostic Explanations): Simplifying Complex Predictions

LIME explains individual predictions by training a simple, interpretable model (such as linear regression) locally around a specific instance. This approach approximates the complex model behavior locally, making it easier to understand specific predictions.

How LIME Works

- **Step 1**: For a given instance, LIME perturbs the data to create variations of the instance.
- **Step 2**: The model predicts outcomes for each variation.
- **Step 3**: LIME fits a simple interpretable model (e.g., linear) on these variations, identifying the features most responsible for the original instance's prediction.

Example of LIME in Practice

In a credit scoring model, LIME can explain why a particular applicant was denied a loan. By creating variations of this applicant's profile, LIME shows which factors, like "low income" or "high debt-to-income ratio," had the greatest influence on the denial decision.

Advantages of LIME

- **Model-Agnostic**: Works with any model, providing flexibility.
- **Local Interpretability**: Ideal for explaining specific predictions, helping stakeholders understand individual outcomes.

Best Practices for Using LIME

- **Use for Complex Models**: Apply LIME when explaining predictions from complex models like neural networks or ensemble methods.

- **Combine with SHAP for Completeness**: LIME and SHAP are complementary; use LIME for case-specific explanations and SHAP for a broader understanding.

6. Surrogate Models: Building Interpretable Proxies for Complex Models

A surrogate model is a simpler model trained to mimic the behavior of a more complex model, providing interpretable approximations of the original model's predictions. Surrogate models are helpful when the primary model is too complex to interpret directly.

Steps to Create a Surrogate Model

1. **Train the Complex Model**: Develop the primary model to achieve high accuracy.
2. **Generate Predictions**: Use the primary model to make predictions on the training or validation set.
3. **Train the Surrogate Model**: Train a simpler model (e.g., decision tree) to approximate the primary model's predictions.

Example of a Surrogate Model in Healthcare

In a healthcare setting, a complex deep learning model might predict patient risk, but its black-box nature complicates interpretation. Training a decision tree surrogate model based on the deep learning model's predictions provides a more understandable framework that identifies key risk factors.

Advantages of Surrogate Models

- **Simplified Explanations**: Surrogate models offer insights into complex models without compromising too much on accuracy.

- **Flexible Approach**: Applicable to any black-box model, from neural networks to ensemble methods.

Best Practices for Using Surrogate Models

- **Balance Accuracy and Interpretability**: Ensure the surrogate model captures the complex model's behavior reasonably well while maintaining simplicity.
- **Use for Auditing**: Surrogate models can validate that the primary model's predictions align with expected patterns, making them useful for compliance.

7. Interpreting Results with Counterfactual Explanations

Counterfactual explanations identify the minimum changes needed in feature values to alter a model's prediction. This technique is particularly useful in fields where stakeholders want to understand actionable changes that could influence outcomes.

Example of Counterfactual Explanation in Loan Approval

In a loan application model, a counterfactual explanation might reveal that increasing the applicant's income by $5,000 or reducing debt by $10,000 would lead to a loan approval. This approach provides applicants with actionable steps to potentially change the outcome.

Benefits of Counterfactual Explanations

- **Actionable Insights**: Counterfactuals show what changes are needed for a different prediction, making them useful for customer feedback or strategic adjustments.
- **Clear Communication**: By specifying required changes, counterfactuals make it easier for non-technical

stakeholders to understand how they could impact predictions.

Best Practices for Using Counterfactuals

- **Limit Changes to Feasible Adjustments**: Focus on counterfactuals that involve realistic, actionable adjustments.
- **Validate for Fairness**: Ensure counterfactuals do not suggest biased or unreasonable changes, maintaining ethical standards.

Conclusion

Model interpretability is a cornerstone of responsible machine learning, allowing data scientists to create transparent, trustworthy models that stakeholders can understand and rely upon. Techniques like feature importance, SHAP, LIME, surrogate models, and counterfactual explanations offer various approaches to make models understandable, balancing complexity with clarity. By incorporating interpretability into the evaluation and optimization process, machine learning practitioners can ensure that their models not only perform well but also align with organizational, ethical, and regulatory standards. As we continue, these interpretability techniques will be essential for creating robust models that not only predict effectively but also empower data-driven, transparent decision-making.

Chapter 7: Deep Learning in Advanced Data Analytics

Practical Steps for Implementing Deep Learning Models for Tasks Like Image Classification and NLP

Deep learning empowers data analysts to handle complex tasks such as image classification and natural language processing, or NLP, achieving remarkable levels of accuracy and efficiency. However, implementing these models successfully requires an understanding of the right neural network structures, careful data preparation, and specialized tools. This chapter provides a step-by-step guide to building and deploying deep learning models for tasks like image classification and NLP.

Implementing Image Classification Models with Convolutional Neural Networks (CNNs)

Image classification is a popular application of deep learning, where Convolutional Neural Networks, or CNNs, are used to categorize images. CNNs are ideal for this task because they can capture spatial details and hierarchies in images.

Step-by-Step Guide for Image Classification

Step 1: Prepare the Dataset

1. **Gather Images**: Collect labeled images relevant to the classification task, with each label representing a category, like "cat" or "dog."
2. **Split the Dataset**: Divide the images into training, validation, and test sets, commonly splitting with 70% for training, 15% for validation, and 15% for testing.

3. **Data Augmentation**: Apply techniques such as rotation, flipping, and scaling to expand the training set and improve the model's ability to generalize.

Example: For a dataset with 5,000 labeled animal images, using data augmentation to create variations will strengthen model robustness.

Step 2: Design the CNN Architecture

1. **Input Layer**: Set the input layer to match the image size, such as 128 by 128 pixels for RGB images.
2. **Convolutional Layers**: Add multiple convolutional layers with filters, or kernels, to capture image features like edges and textures. Increase the number of filters in deeper layers to capture more complex patterns.
3. **Pooling Layers**: Insert pooling layers, such as max pooling, after convolutional layers to reduce dimensions while keeping essential features.
4. **Fully Connected Layers**: Flatten the output and add dense layers for classification.
5. **Output Layer**: Use a softmax output layer, with a node for each class, like "cat," "dog," and "rabbit."

Step 3: Compile and Train the Model

1. **Compile the Model**: Choose a loss function like categorical cross-entropy for multi-class classification and select an optimizer such as Adam.
2. **Train the Model**: Train the model on the training set while using the validation set to monitor its performance. Adjust batch size and epoch settings based on dataset size and hardware capacity.

Step 4: Evaluate the Model on the Test Set

1. **Accuracy and Loss**: Measure accuracy and loss on the test set to assess generalization capability.
2. **Confusion Matrix**: Use a confusion matrix to visualize classification accuracy across categories and identify areas for improvement.

Step 5: Deploy the Model

1. **Save the Model**: Export the trained model for deployment or integration into applications.
2. **Inference**: Set up code for real-time inference, allowing the model to classify new images as they come in.

Implementing Natural Language Processing (NLP) Models with Recurrent Neural Networks (RNNs)

Recurrent Neural Networks, or RNNs, are effective for natural language processing tasks, such as sentiment analysis, language translation, and text classification, thanks to their ability to capture sequential information.

Step-by-Step Guide for Text Classification Using RNNs

Step 1: Prepare the Text Dataset

1. **Gather Data**: Collect labeled text samples, such as customer reviews labeled as "positive" or "negative."
2. **Tokenize and Clean**: Tokenize text to convert words into numerical format and clean by removing stop words, punctuation, and special characters.
3. **Padding**: Use padding to ensure that all sequences are the same length, which allows for batch processing.

Step 2: Design the RNN Architecture

1. **Embedding Layer**: Use an embedding layer to convert words into dense vectors, capturing semantic meaning.
2. **Recurrent Layers**: Add recurrent layers, like Long Short-Term Memory (LSTM) or Gated Recurrent Units (GRU), to capture sequence dependencies.
3. **Fully Connected Layers**: Flatten the output and add dense layers for classification.

Step 3: Compile and Train the Model

1. **Compile the Model**: Choose a loss function, such as binary cross-entropy for binary classification, and an optimizer like Adam.
2. **Train the Model**: Train the model on the training set and validate on the validation set to ensure optimal performance.

Step 4: Evaluate the Model on the Test Set

1. **Performance Metrics**: Assess the model's accuracy, precision, recall, and F1-score.
2. **Confusion Matrix**: Visualize misclassifications using a confusion matrix to spot areas for potential improvement.

Step 5: Deploy the Model

1. **Save and Export**: Export the model for deployment.
2. **Inference**: Set up a real-time inference process to allow users to input text and receive predictions.

Practical Tips for Training Deep Learning Models

Training deep learning models can be challenging, but these tips can help maximize performance:

1. **Regularization Techniques**: Use dropout layers to reduce overfitting by randomly disabling neurons during training, particularly in large networks.
2. **Early Stopping**: Monitor validation performance and stop training when performance plateaus to prevent overfitting and save time.
3. **Data Augmentation**: Apply data augmentation to images to increase dataset size and variety, enhancing the model's ability to generalize.
4. **Hyperparameter Tuning**: Experiment with learning rate, batch size, and layer configuration to find the optimal model setup.

Real-World Applications of Image Classification and NLP in Analytics

Deep learning applications are widely used across industries, turning complex data into actionable insights.

Image Classification Applications

- **Healthcare**: CNNs are used to analyze medical images like X-rays and MRIs for disease detection.
- **Retail**: Image classification helps with product identification in inventory systems, improving catalog organization.

NLP Applications

- **Customer Sentiment Analysis**: NLP models can analyze customer feedback and social media posts to detect trends in sentiment, guiding marketing strategies.

- **Chatbots and Virtual Assistants**: RNN-based models allow chatbots to understand and respond to user questions, improving customer support.

Conclusion

Implementing deep learning models for tasks such as image classification and NLP requires selecting the appropriate neural network architectures, preparing data effectively, and using efficient training practices. Convolutional Neural Networks are particularly suited to image tasks, while Recurrent Neural Networks are optimal for processing sequential text data. By following these practical steps, data scientists can successfully build, evaluate, and deploy deep learning models that drive meaningful insights and solve real-world challenges. As we continue, developing these deep learning skills will be essential to unlocking the value of unstructured data and driving innovation in the data analytics space.

Real-World Scenarios Where Deep Learning Outperforms Traditional Machine Learning Models

Deep learning has gained prominence for its ability to process and learn from vast amounts of complex, unstructured data—something traditional machine learning models struggle with. By leveraging layered architectures like neural networks, Convolutional Neural Networks (CNNs), and Recurrent Neural Networks (RNNs), deep learning models can identify patterns and make predictions in scenarios where traditional models fall short. This chapter explores real-world scenarios across industries where deep learning significantly outperforms traditional machine learning models.

1. Image Recognition and Object Detection in Healthcare

In healthcare, deep learning's image recognition capabilities have transformed the analysis of medical images, such as X-rays, CT scans, and MRIs. Traditional machine learning models are limited in image analysis, as they rely on predefined features, while deep learning automatically extracts relevant features, capturing complex details in images.

Example: Disease Detection in Radiology

- **Traditional Model Limitations**: Traditional machine learning models require manual feature extraction, which depends heavily on expert knowledge and is time-consuming.
- **Deep Learning Advantage**: CNNs automatically identify features such as tumor shapes, densities, and textures in radiological images, detecting diseases like cancer, pneumonia, and fractures with high accuracy.

Real-World Impact: CNNs are used in diagnostic tools to assist radiologists by highlighting areas of concern, reducing diagnostic time and improving accuracy in early disease detection.

2. Natural Language Processing (NLP) for Sentiment Analysis and Language Translation

Natural Language Processing (NLP) tasks, such as sentiment analysis and language translation, are essential for applications like social media monitoring, customer service, and content localization. Traditional models, like Naive Bayes and Support

Vector Machines (SVM), are limited in their ability to handle long-range dependencies and context in text.

Example: Sentiment Analysis in Social Media Monitoring

- **Traditional Model Limitations**: Machine learning models like logistic regression and Naive Bayes analyze sentiment at a basic level but struggle with nuanced language, sarcasm, and context.
- **Deep Learning Advantage**: Recurrent Neural Networks (RNNs), particularly Long Short-Term Memory (LSTM) networks, excel at capturing sequential dependencies, understanding context, and processing long text sequences, improving sentiment classification accuracy.

Real-World Impact: Deep learning NLP models provide more accurate sentiment insights, enabling companies to gauge customer sentiment accurately, react promptly to crises, and refine marketing strategies.

Example: Language Translation

- **Traditional Model Limitations**: Rule-based or statistical machine translation models are limited by vocabulary size and cannot capture complex grammatical rules and context.
- **Deep Learning Advantage**: Neural Machine Translation (NMT) with attention mechanisms allows deep learning models to translate text accurately, considering context, grammar, and linguistic nuances.

Real-World Impact: NMT powers applications like Google Translate, enabling real-time language translation and supporting communication across language barriers in education, travel, and international business.

3. Image Classification in Retail and E-commerce

In retail, visual search and product categorization are increasingly essential as companies seek to improve user experience and inventory management. Traditional models struggle with the complexity of high-dimensional image data, requiring manual feature engineering and extensive pre-processing.

Example: Product Image Classification and Tagging

- **Traditional Model Limitations**: Machine learning models require human intervention to select features such as color and texture, which can be labor-intensive and error-prone.

- **Deep Learning Advantage**: CNNs automatically extract and learn complex visual features, enabling accurate classification of products based on attributes like color, style, and brand.

Real-World Impact: Deep learning-powered visual search engines let customers search for products by uploading images, improving user experience and increasing conversion rates. Retailers can also tag products automatically, streamlining catalog organization and search functionality.

4. Fraud Detection in Finance

Fraud detection in financial transactions is a high-stakes application requiring sophisticated models that can identify fraudulent patterns in real time. Traditional machine learning models are often limited by their reliance on manually engineered features and their inability to detect complex, evolving patterns.

Example: Detecting Anomalous Transactions

- **Traditional Model Limitations**: Models like decision trees or logistic regression rely on pre-defined rules and engineered features, which can struggle to adapt to new, sophisticated fraud tactics.
- **Deep Learning Advantage**: Deep learning models, such as autoencoders and LSTMs, excel at anomaly detection, identifying subtle, evolving patterns that indicate fraud. By learning directly from transaction data, these models are better at detecting outliers and adapting to new fraudulent behaviors.

Real-World Impact: Banks and financial institutions use deep learning models for real-time fraud detection, reducing losses and protecting customers from fraud by automatically flagging suspicious transactions.

5. Autonomous Driving and Object Detection in Transportation

Autonomous driving requires accurate object detection, classification, and tracking of other vehicles, pedestrians, and road signs. Traditional machine learning models are limited by their inability to process complex, high-dimensional image and video data efficiently.

Example: Object Detection for Autonomous Vehicles

- **Traditional Model Limitations**: Conventional object detection models, like HOG-SVM, struggle to handle dynamic environments with multiple objects and varying lighting conditions.

- **Deep Learning Advantage**: CNNs and their advanced architectures (e.g., YOLO and Faster R-CNN) excel at processing high-dimensional visual data, detecting multiple objects in real-time and capturing complex spatial relationships between objects.

Real-World Impact: Deep learning is the backbone of autonomous vehicle perception systems, enabling vehicles to detect objects, recognize road signs, and make split-second decisions to ensure passenger and pedestrian safety.

6. Voice Recognition and Speech-to-Text in Consumer Technology

Voice recognition is a rapidly growing area in consumer technology, powering virtual assistants like Siri, Alexa, and Google Assistant. Traditional models for voice recognition struggle with accents, background noise, and continuous speech, making them less reliable.

Example: Speech-to-Text for Virtual Assistants

- **Traditional Model Limitations**: Traditional models, like Hidden Markov Models (HMMs), rely on phoneme matching and predefined dictionaries, which are inflexible and less accurate for diverse speech patterns.
- **Deep Learning Advantage**: Deep learning models, especially RNNs and transformers, handle complex audio patterns, processing contextual information and enabling continuous speech recognition.

Real-World Impact: Deep learning has vastly improved the accuracy of speech-to-text systems, allowing virtual assistants to understand voice commands more accurately, enhancing the user experience and enabling hands-free device control.

7. Predictive Maintenance in Manufacturing

Predictive maintenance uses data from sensors and machines to predict equipment failures before they occur. Traditional models often struggle to capture the complexities of high-dimensional sensor data and dependencies over time.

Example: Failure Prediction for Industrial Machinery

- **Traditional Model Limitations**: Machine learning models like logistic regression require extensive feature engineering to capture signals from sensor data, limiting their predictive power.
- **Deep Learning Advantage**: Deep learning models, particularly RNNs and LSTMs, excel at processing time-series data from sensors. They capture temporal patterns in sensor readings that indicate wear or malfunction, predicting failures more accurately.

Real-World Impact: Predictive maintenance systems powered by deep learning prevent costly downtime and extend the lifespan of industrial equipment, resulting in substantial savings for manufacturers.

8. Recommender Systems in E-commerce and Streaming Services

Recommender systems play a vital role in e-commerce, streaming services, and social media by personalizing content for users. Traditional collaborative filtering approaches can only capture basic user-item interactions and are limited in scalability.

Example: Content and Product Recommendations

- **Traditional Model Limitations**: Collaborative filtering models struggle with the "cold start" problem, where new users and items lack sufficient data, and cannot capture deep patterns in user preferences.
- **Deep Learning Advantage**: Neural Collaborative Filtering and deep learning-based recommendation engines combine user behavior, content features, and context to provide personalized recommendations. They excel at capturing non-linear relationships and adapting to changes in user preferences.

Real-World Impact: Streaming services like Netflix and Spotify use deep learning for personalized recommendations, enhancing customer satisfaction by providing relevant content, increasing engagement, and reducing churn.

9. Weather Prediction and Climate Modeling

Weather prediction relies on processing large volumes of meteorological data, such as temperature, pressure, and satellite images. Traditional statistical models are limited in capturing the non-linear, interdependent relationships in weather patterns.

Example: Short-Term Weather Forecasting

- **Traditional Model Limitations**: Statistical models rely on past patterns, but they struggle with complex, multi-dimensional data and are less effective in dynamic weather conditions.

- **Deep Learning Advantage**: CNNs and RNNs process multi-dimensional, temporal data, making them well-suited for weather prediction. CNNs analyze satellite images, while RNNs model time-series data from sensors and past weather records.

Real-World Impact: Deep learning models enable more accurate and timely weather predictions, aiding in disaster preparedness and reducing economic losses from extreme weather events.

Conclusion

Deep learning significantly outperforms traditional machine learning models in scenarios involving complex, high-dimensional, and unstructured data, such as images, text, and time-series data. From healthcare diagnostics to personalized recommendations and autonomous driving, deep learning models provide advanced pattern recognition and predictive capabilities, driving innovation and insights across industries. Mastering these deep learning applications enables data scientists to tackle sophisticated problems, creating opportunities for transformative impact in advanced data analytics. As technology continues to evolve, deep learning will remain a cornerstone of data-driven decision-making, pushing the boundaries of what's possible in analytics.

Chapter 8: Time Series and Sequential Data Analysis

Techniques for Analyzing Time-Dependent Data, Forecasting Trends, and Recognizing Patterns

Time series and sequential data analysis are critical for uncovering trends and patterns over time. Whether you're forecasting stock prices, analyzing customer behavior, or monitoring sensor data, time-dependent data offers powerful insights for decision-making and planning. This chapter delves into key techniques for analyzing time series and sequential data, focusing on forecasting trends, recognizing patterns, and detecting anomalies.

1. Introduction to Time Series and Sequential Data

Time series data consists of sequential observations taken at regular time intervals, like daily, monthly, or yearly. In contrast, sequential data includes any ordered data, such as text sequences or clickstreams, where the sequence matters even if the time intervals vary.

Key Characteristics of Time Series Data

- **Trend**: The overall direction of the data—whether it's increasing, decreasing, or stable.
- **Seasonality**: Repeating patterns or cycles at regular intervals, such as daily, weekly, or annually.
- **Noise**: Random fluctuations that obscure trends and patterns.
- **Stationarity**: Indicates whether the statistical properties (like mean or variance) of the series remain

constant over time. Many forecasting models require stationary data.

Applications of Time Series Analysis

- **Financial Markets**: Predicting stock prices and economic indicators.
- **Supply Chain**: Demand forecasting for inventory management.
- **Healthcare**: Monitoring patient vitals to detect patterns or anomalies.
- **Utilities**: Analyzing energy usage for demand forecasting and optimization.

2. Preparing Data for Time Series Analysis

Effective time series analysis begins with proper data preprocessing to handle missing values, reduce noise, and ensure the data is suitable for modeling.

Common Preprocessing Techniques

- **Handling Missing Data**: Use methods like interpolation or forward and backward filling to maintain continuity.
- **Smoothing**: Techniques like moving averages reduce noise, highlighting trends and patterns.
- **Differencing**: Subtract consecutive observations to remove trends and achieve stationarity, which is crucial for certain models.

Example: A 7-day moving average smooths daily sales data, helping businesses identify weekly trends without being distracted by day-to-day fluctuations.

3. Analyzing Trends and Decomposing Time Series Data

Decomposing time series data into components—trend, seasonality, and residuals—helps isolate patterns and prepare for forecasting.

Decomposition Methods

- **Additive Decomposition**: Assumes the series is the sum of its components.
- **Multiplicative Decomposition**: Assumes the components multiply together, often used when seasonal variations grow with the trend.

Example: By decomposing a monthly sales dataset, businesses can identify long-term growth trends, seasonal peaks, and random fluctuations.

4. Time Series Forecasting Techniques

Forecasting is the primary goal of time series analysis. Different models cater to various data types and forecasting horizons.

4.1 ARIMA (Autoregressive Integrated Moving Average)

- Combines autoregression, differencing, and moving averages to model stationary data.
- Effective for capturing dependencies in data over time.

4.2 SARIMA (Seasonal ARIMA)

- Extends ARIMA by including seasonal components, making it ideal for data with repeating cycles, such as monthly sales peaks.

4.3 Exponential Smoothing (ETS)

- Models that use weighted averages to forecast trends and seasonality.

- Includes variants like Holt-Winters, which accounts for both trend and seasonality.

5. Machine Learning Approaches to Time Series Forecasting

Traditional methods like ARIMA work well for simpler patterns, but machine learning can handle complex datasets with additional variables.

5.1 Tree-Based Models

- **Random Forests** and **Gradient Boosting** capture non-linear relationships.
- Useful for combining time series features with external factors like weather or marketing campaigns.

5.2 Neural Networks

- **Recurrent Neural Networks (RNNs)** and **LSTMs** excel at learning long-term dependencies in sequential data.
- Often used in stock price prediction, where historical prices influence future trends.

6. Recognizing Patterns and Detecting Anomalies

Beyond forecasting, pattern recognition helps identify seasonal cycles and unexpected deviations.

Anomaly Detection

- **Moving Average with Control Limits**: Flags data points outside predefined limits as anomalies.
- **Isolation Forest**: Identifies outliers by isolating points that deviate from the main pattern.

Seasonal Pattern Detection

- Recognizing recurring patterns, like increased sales during holidays, allows businesses to plan proactively.

7. Evaluating Time Series Models

To ensure accuracy, use evaluation metrics designed for time-ordered data.

Common Metrics

- **Mean Absolute Error (MAE)**: Measures average prediction errors.
- **Root Mean Squared Error (RMSE)**: Penalizes larger errors more heavily than MAE.
- **Mean Absolute Percentage Error (MAPE)**: Expresses error as a percentage of actual values, enabling comparison across datasets.

Conclusion

Time series and sequential data analysis provide powerful tools for understanding and forecasting trends, identifying patterns, and making proactive decisions. By mastering techniques ranging from traditional models like ARIMA to advanced machine learning approaches like LSTMs, professionals can unlock valuable insights in fields ranging from finance to healthcare. These methods are essential for building accurate, actionable models that drive real-world results.

Applications in Finance, IoT, and Retail Analytics

Time series and sequential data analysis have broad applications across industries that rely on real-time and historical data to drive insights and decision-making. In finance, Internet of Things (IoT), and retail, analyzing time-dependent data is critical for forecasting trends, optimizing operations, and enhancing customer experiences. This chapter explores real-world applications of time series and sequential data analysis in these three sectors, demonstrating how organizations can leverage these techniques for actionable insights.

1. Time Series Analysis in Finance

In finance, time series analysis is essential for forecasting stock prices, assessing economic indicators, predicting market trends, and managing risk. Financial data are often highly volatile, seasonal, and impacted by external factors like economic events, making it a perfect fit for time series techniques that handle complex temporal patterns.

Key Applications in Finance

- **Stock Price Prediction**: Time series models such as ARIMA, LSTM, and SARIMA are widely used for stock price forecasting. They help traders and investors make informed decisions by analyzing historical stock prices, volumes, and economic indicators.
    - o **Example**: LSTM networks, which capture long-term dependencies in sequential data, are applied to predict stock prices by analyzing past prices, volume, and market sentiment.
- **Algorithmic Trading**: Algorithmic trading systems leverage high-frequency data and time series models to identify trading opportunities, making quick buy/sell decisions based on real-time data.
    - o **Example**: Gradient Boosting models can analyze high-frequency data, such as second-by-second

price changes, to spot short-term trends and execute trades automatically.

- **Risk Management and Volatility Forecasting**: Financial institutions use time series models to assess risk by predicting market volatility. Models like GARCH (Generalized Autoregressive Conditional Heteroskedasticity) specifically model changing volatility patterns.
  - o **Example**: Banks use GARCH models to assess currency volatility, which informs foreign exchange strategies and mitigates risks from exchange rate fluctuations.
- **Credit Scoring and Loan Default Prediction**: Time series analysis of credit card usage and loan repayment histories helps predict loan default risks, assisting banks in credit risk assessment.
  - o **Example**: Analyzing payment behavior over time, banks apply logistic regression or LSTM models to identify customers likely to default, enabling proactive risk management.

Real-World Impact: By forecasting stock trends, managing risk, and automating trades, financial institutions optimize decision-making, increase profitability, and manage risks effectively.

2. Time Series and Sequential Data in Internet of Things (IoT)

IoT devices generate continuous streams of time-stamped data from sensors and systems, often deployed in industries like manufacturing, healthcare, energy, and smart cities. Analyzing this data helps organizations monitor assets, perform predictive maintenance, optimize energy use, and enhance safety.

Key Applications in IoT

- **Predictive Maintenance in Manufacturing**: Time series analysis of sensor data from machines identifies early signs of wear or malfunction, allowing for maintenance before a failure occurs.
  - o **Example**: LSTM and anomaly detection models monitor variables like temperature, vibration, and pressure in factory machines, predicting failures and reducing unplanned downtime.
- **Energy Usage Optimization in Smart Grids**: Utility companies analyze time series data on electricity consumption to balance supply and demand, prevent outages, and promote efficient energy use.
  - o **Example**: Seasonal ARIMA models forecast energy consumption, enabling utilities to adjust power distribution during peak and off-peak hours and prevent grid overload.
- **Anomaly Detection in Smart Cities**: Time series analysis of IoT data from traffic sensors, CCTV, and environmental sensors helps detect anomalies, such as unusual traffic congestion or air quality issues.
  - o **Example**: Anomaly detection models can identify unusual spikes in traffic flow, which can inform

traffic rerouting strategies and reduce congestion in real-time.

- **Health Monitoring in Wearable Devices**: Time series data from wearable devices, like heart rate and activity level, allow for continuous health monitoring, providing valuable insights into a person's health trends.
  - o **Example**: Anomaly detection and RNNs analyze heart rate data to detect irregular patterns, alerting users to potential health risks such as arrhythmias.

Real-World Impact: By leveraging time series analysis, IoT applications improve operational efficiency, enhance safety, reduce costs, and empower proactive decision-making.

3. Sequential Data Analysis in Retail Analytics

In retail, analyzing sequential data such as purchase history, customer visits, and transaction trends enables companies to personalize customer experiences, optimize inventory, and drive sales. Time series analysis is crucial for demand forecasting, customer behavior analysis, and supply chain management.

Key Applications in Retail Analytics

- **Demand Forecasting**: Retailers use time series models to forecast demand for products, helping with inventory management, replenishment planning, and minimizing stockouts or overstocking.
  - o **Example**: Seasonal ARIMA and Exponential Smoothing models predict seasonal peaks in

demand (e.g., holiday shopping season), allowing retailers to stock appropriately.

- **Customer Behavior Analysis and Segmentation**: Sequential data analysis of customer interactions, such as transaction history, browsing behavior, and purchase patterns, provides insights into customer preferences.
  - o **Example**: RNNs analyze purchase history sequences to identify loyal customers and segment them based on purchasing patterns, enabling personalized marketing and rewards.
- **Sales Trend Analysis**: Time series analysis of sales data helps identify long-term and seasonal sales trends, empowering retailers to adapt strategies and product offerings.
  - o **Example**: Retailers use decomposition techniques to separate trends, seasonality, and noise in monthly sales data, identifying growth opportunities and areas for improvement.
- **Inventory and Supply Chain Optimization**: Time series analysis allows retailers to optimize their inventory by predicting lead times and sales cycles, reducing costs and ensuring stock availability.
  - o **Example**: SARIMA models forecast restocking needs for high-demand items, reducing the risk of stockouts and improving supply chain efficiency.

Real-World Impact: Time series and sequential data analysis in retail enhances demand forecasting, personalizes customer experiences, optimizes inventory, and ultimately boosts profitability.

4. Practical Example of Time Series Analysis in Finance, IoT, and Retail

To illustrate the application of time series analysis across these sectors, let's examine a practical example:

Case Study: Predicting and Managing Demand Peaks Across Finance, IoT, and Retail

A large retail chain with connected IoT-enabled warehouses and distribution centers wants to prepare for the holiday season. The goal is to accurately forecast product demand, optimize inventory across locations, and secure additional funding to support increased sales.

Finance Application: Stock Price and Risk Management

- The company uses LSTM models to analyze the seasonal patterns in its stock prices during past holiday seasons, forecasting the expected impact on its stock value and allowing it to manage investor expectations.

IoT Application: Inventory Optimization with Predictive Maintenance

- IoT devices on warehouse equipment (e.g., forklifts and conveyor belts) continuously monitor usage data. Anomaly detection models predict when machines are likely to require maintenance, reducing the chance of equipment failures during peak demand.

Retail Application: Demand Forecasting and Customer Behavior Analysis

- ARIMA and SARIMA models forecast holiday demand for top products, allowing the retailer to optimize stock levels. Additionally, analyzing customer transaction sequences using RNNs identifies which customer segments are likely to increase their purchases, enabling targeted marketing campaigns.

Outcome: By applying time series analysis across finance, IoT, and retail, the retailer can prepare for demand surges, maintain efficient operations, and enhance customer satisfaction, leading to a successful holiday season.

5. Choosing the Right Time Series Model for Industry Applications

Selecting the right model depends on the data characteristics, the application, and the business goals. Here is a summary of recommended models by application:

- **Finance**: Use ARIMA for traditional trend forecasting, LSTMs for stock price prediction and sequential dependencies, and GARCH for volatility analysis.
- **IoT**: Use Exponential Smoothing and SARIMA for demand patterns, LSTMs for time-dependent predictive maintenance, and anomaly detection models for real-time monitoring.
- **Retail**: Use SARIMA and Exponential Smoothing for seasonal demand forecasting, RNNs for customer purchase sequence analysis, and time series decomposition for sales trend analysis.

Conclusion

Time series and sequential data analysis play a transformative role in finance, IoT, and retail analytics. Each of these sectors benefits from leveraging historical and real-time data to make informed predictions, optimize operations, and enhance customer experiences. By using time series models like ARIMA, LSTMs, and Exponential Smoothing, organizations can forecast trends, detect anomalies, and adapt strategies to changing patterns. As we continue, these applications will become increasingly sophisticated, supporting data-driven decision-making and driving innovation in advanced data analytics.

Methods for Evaluating Time Series Models and Improving Forecast Accuracy

Time series forecasting models are essential tools for predicting future trends and enabling proactive planning. To be effective, these models need rigorous evaluation and regular improvements to their accuracy. In this chapter, we'll explore key metrics and methods for assessing time series model performance, along with techniques to refine forecast accuracy through model tuning, data preparation, and advanced modeling.

1. Evaluation Metrics for Time Series Forecasting

Choosing appropriate evaluation metrics is crucial for accurately measuring how well a time series model performs. Common metrics help quantify the difference between predicted values and actual values, providing insights into forecast quality.

- **Mean Absolute Error (MAE)**: This metric calculates the average of absolute differences between predicted values and actual values. It gives a straightforward interpretation of the average error magnitude. Lower MAE values indicate a better model fit, offering an easily understood measure of forecast accuracy.
- **Mean Squared Error (MSE) and Root Mean Squared Error (RMSE)**: MSE measures the average squared difference between predicted and actual values, while RMSE takes the square root of MSE to keep results in the same unit as the original data. These metrics emphasize larger errors, making them useful when minimizing large deviations is important.
- **Mean Absolute Percentage Error (MAPE)**: This metric calculates the average percentage error, which is helpful when comparing forecast accuracy across different datasets. However, MAPE may not be ideal for series with values near zero.
- **Mean Absolute Scaled Error (MASE)**: MASE provides a standardized accuracy measure by comparing model errors to those from a naive benchmark model. Values below 1 indicate that the model performs better than the benchmark.

Choosing the Right Metric: Use MAE and RMSE when error magnitude is a priority, MAPE for comparisons across scales with non-zero values, and MASE for standardized comparisons across different time series.

2. Backtesting: Validating Time Series Models with Historical Data

Backtesting is the practice of testing a model's performance on historical data by splitting it into training and testing sets. This process helps evaluate how well the model generalizes to unseen data.

- **Fixed Origin Backtesting**: In this approach, you divide data into a single training and testing period. For example, in a dataset covering five years, the first four years can be used for training, and the last year for testing. This approach is suitable for one-time forecasts.

- **Rolling Window Backtesting**: This method involves training the model on a fixed window of past data, then shifting the window forward for each forecast. For example, you might use 12 months of sales data to predict the next month, repeating this for each new period. Rolling windows provide multiple validation points, testing how adaptable the model is over time.

- **Expanding Window Backtesting**: Similar to rolling windows, but here, the training set grows with each new forecast, adding more historical data over time. For example, start with six months of data, then add each subsequent month to the training set before forecasting.

Best Practices for Backtesting: Select a window that matches the forecast horizon, assess performance over multiple periods, and use both rolling and expanding windows as needed to understand the model's adaptability.

3. Techniques for Improving Forecast Accuracy

Improving forecast accuracy often involves optimizing data preparation, fine-tuning model parameters, and exploring advanced modeling techniques.

- **Data Preprocessing**:
  - o **Smoothing and Denoising**: Techniques like moving averages reduce random fluctuations, allowing the model to focus on meaningful patterns.
  - o **Differencing**: Differencing removes trends and seasonality to make the series stationary, which is often necessary for models like ARIMA.
  - o **Seasonal Adjustment**: For consistently seasonal data, remove seasonal components so the model can focus on underlying trends.
- **Hyperparameter Tuning**:
  - o **Grid Search**: This method tests different combinations of parameters exhaustively to find the best configuration.
  - o **Random Search**: Randomly selects parameter combinations, making it less exhaustive but faster than grid search.
  - o **Bayesian Optimization**: This approach uses a probabilistic model to balance exploration of new parameter values with exploitation of known values, improving efficiency.
- **Ensemble Methods**:

- Bagging: Creates multiple models from different data samples and averages their predictions to reduce variance.
- Boosting: Trains models sequentially, where each model learns from the errors of the previous one, boosting overall accuracy.
- Hybrid Models: Combines different model types, such as using ARIMA for long-term trends and LSTM for short-term fluctuations, to capture both stable and dynamic patterns.

4. Advanced Forecasting Techniques

For complex time series, advanced methods offer improved accuracy by capturing intricate relationships within the data.

- **Recurrent Neural Networks (RNNs) and Long Short-Term Memory (LSTM)**: These models excel at sequential data analysis, handling long-term dependencies in time series data, making them well-suited for stock prices, energy demand, and sales forecasting. Adjust model depth, dropout rate, and unit count to prevent overfitting.
- **Prophet**: Developed by Facebook, Prophet is ideal for time series with strong seasonal patterns. It handles missing data, outliers, and seasonal trends efficiently, making it a good choice for business metrics like sales or web traffic.
- **Transfer Learning in Time Series**: Transfer learning applies knowledge from one domain to another, reducing the need for large amounts of data in each new

setting. In time series, a model trained on data from one region or product can be fine-tuned for another, enhancing forecast performance while minimizing data requirements.

5. Model Monitoring and Continuous Improvement

Once deployed, a time series model requires regular monitoring to maintain accuracy in dynamic environments.

- **Drift Detection**: Use statistical tests to detect changes in data patterns over time, which may signal the need for model retraining.
- **Retraining**: Regularly update the model with the latest data to adapt to shifting patterns.
- **Continuous Backtesting**: Periodically re-evaluate the model on recent data to ensure that it continues to perform well over time.

Conclusion

Evaluating and refining time series models requires a mix of appropriate metrics, validation techniques, and continuous improvement strategies. By using data preprocessing, tuning, ensemble methods, and advanced techniques like LSTM and Prophet, analysts can build more accurate and reliable forecasts. Continuous model monitoring ensures relevance in changing environments, empowering organizations to make proactive and data-driven decisions. As time series modeling evolves, these techniques will be essential for creating robust, high-performing models that support strategic planning across industries.

Chapter 9: Data Ethics and Responsible Analytics

Understanding Ethical Implications in Data Analytics and AI

As data analytics and AI become increasingly embedded in everyday life, the need for ethical practices in handling data and making decisions based on analytics has never been more critical. Ethical data use ensures fairness, protects privacy, builds trust, and mitigates the risk of harmful consequences that could arise from biased algorithms, misuse of personal data, and lack of transparency. This chapter explores the core ethical considerations in data analytics and AI, providing a foundation for responsible practices that respect user rights and promote fairness.

1. The Importance of Data Ethics in Analytics and AI

Data ethics is a framework of principles guiding the responsible collection, processing, and use of data. Ethical practices in data analytics ensure that individuals' rights are respected, decisions are fair, and outcomes are transparent. Misuse of data can lead to reputational damage, loss of customer trust, and even legal consequences.

Key Principles of Data Ethics

- **Transparency**: Individuals should understand how their data is used, and organizations should be open about their data practices.
- **Fairness**: Models and algorithms should avoid bias and ensure equitable treatment across all demographic groups.

- **Privacy**: Data must be handled responsibly to protect personal information, ensuring compliance with data protection laws.
- **Accountability**: Organizations and data scientists should take responsibility for the consequences of their data practices, whether intended or unintended.

Case Example: Importance of Data Ethics in Healthcare

In healthcare, algorithms are used to allocate resources, diagnose diseases, and recommend treatments. Ethical lapses, such as biased algorithms that underdiagnose certain groups, could lead to inadequate care for those populations. Ethical practices ensure that healthcare data is used fairly, safely, and effectively, improving patient outcomes without discrimination.

2. Privacy and Data Protection: Ensuring User Consent and Control

Privacy is a fundamental right, and responsible analytics should prioritize safeguarding individuals' personal information. Privacy is particularly relevant in analytics since data is often collected from sources like social media, mobile apps, and IoT devices, sometimes without full user awareness.

Best Practices for Privacy Protection

- **Informed Consent**: Users must be informed about data collection practices and have the choice to opt in or out, as required by laws like GDPR and CCPA.
- **Data Minimization**: Only collect the data necessary for analysis, reducing exposure to sensitive information.

- **Anonymization and Pseudonymization**: Mask identifiable data where possible to protect individual privacy, especially when sharing datasets with third parties.
- **User Control**: Provide users with control over their data, including options to delete, review, or update personal information.

Example: GDPR Compliance in Data Analytics

Under the European Union's General Data Protection Regulation (GDPR), organizations are legally required to obtain clear consent for data collection and to provide users with access to their data. Non-compliance with GDPR can lead to substantial fines and loss of consumer trust, emphasizing the importance of privacy in analytics.

3. Avoiding Bias and Ensuring Fairness in Data Models

Bias in data or algorithms can lead to unfair treatment of certain groups, resulting in discrimination and unjust outcomes. Ethical analytics should prioritize fairness by identifying and mitigating bias throughout the modeling process, from data collection to model deployment.

Sources of Bias

- **Data Bias**: Historical data may reflect societal biases, such as underrepresentation of certain demographics, which can lead to skewed results.
- **Algorithmic Bias**: Some algorithms amplify bias by overfitting on majority group data or underweighting minority groups.

- **Human Bias**: Unintentional bias introduced during data labeling, model selection, or interpretation of results.

Strategies for Ensuring Fairness

- **Diverse Data Collection**: Ensure the dataset represents a diverse population, reducing the likelihood of underrepresented groups being marginalized.
- **Fairness Metrics**: Use metrics like demographic parity, equal opportunity, and equalized odds to measure and mitigate bias in models.
- **Bias Audits**: Conduct regular audits to check for bias, particularly when deploying models that impact sensitive areas like hiring, lending, and criminal justice.

Case Study: Bias in Credit Scoring Models

Credit scoring algorithms sometimes discriminate against minority groups due to biased historical data, limiting their access to loans and financial services. By implementing fairness metrics and auditing these models, financial institutions can work to ensure that their models make unbiased, fair lending decisions.

---

4. Transparency and Explainability: Building Trust in Analytics and AI

Transparency in data analytics means being open about how data is collected, processed, and used to make decisions. Explainability goes a step further, ensuring that model decisions are understandable to non-experts. Together, transparency and explainability help build trust with users, regulators, and other stakeholders.

Challenges in Transparency and Explainability

- **Complex Models**: Deep learning and ensemble methods are often considered "black boxes" due to their complexity, making it challenging to explain how decisions are made.
- **Interpretability vs. Accuracy Trade-off**: Simple models like linear regression are more interpretable but may lack accuracy compared to complex models. Organizations need to balance this trade-off.
- **Stakeholder Understanding**: Transparency is only effective if explanations are understandable to stakeholders, including those without technical expertise.

Tools and Techniques for Explainability

- **Model-Agnostic Tools**: Techniques like SHAP (SHapley Additive exPlanations) and LIME (Local Interpretable Model-Agnostic Explanations) provide insights into feature importance, making model predictions more interpretable.
- **Surrogate Models**: Create simpler, interpretable models to approximate complex models, helping explain predictions without compromising accuracy.
- **Documentation and Disclosure**: Provide clear documentation and user-friendly explanations of model functions and limitations.

Example: Explainability in Healthcare AI

AI models are increasingly used in healthcare for diagnostics and treatment recommendations. To build trust, doctors and patients need to understand how a model arrived at a particular decision, such as a diagnosis. Using SHAP values or LIME to highlight key factors influencing a model's diagnosis allows medical professionals to validate the AI's recommendations.

5. Accountability and the Role of Human Oversight

Accountability in analytics requires organizations and data professionals to take responsibility for their models' impact, acknowledging potential risks and implementing safeguards to prevent misuse or unintended harm. Human oversight is essential, especially when models are deployed in high-stakes settings.

Key Aspects of Accountability

- **Model Monitoring and Evaluation**: Continuously monitor model performance to ensure it remains fair, accurate, and aligned with ethical standards.
- **Human-in-the-Loop Systems**: Include human oversight in model decision-making, allowing experts to review or override automated decisions, particularly in sensitive areas like hiring and criminal justice.
- **Ethics Committees and Governance**: Establish committees to review and approve data practices, ensuring alignment with ethical standards and organizational values.

Example of Accountability: Human Oversight in Hiring Algorithms

Many companies use AI to screen job applications, but biased algorithms may unfairly disadvantage certain groups.

Implementing a human-in-the-loop process enables recruiters to review and validate AI-based recommendations, preventing biased or discriminatory hiring decisions.

6. Responsible Data Collection and Use

Responsible analytics begins with ethical data collection and use practices, ensuring that data is collected fairly, used responsibly, and respects individuals' rights.

Principles of Responsible Data Collection

- **Purpose Limitation**: Only collect data relevant to the specific analysis, avoiding unrelated or excessive data collection.
- **Honest Communication**: Clearly explain why data is being collected and how it will be used, building trust with users.
- **Data Longevity and Disposal**: Retain data only as long as necessary, implementing secure disposal methods once data is no longer needed.

Example: Purpose Limitation in Retail Analytics

In retail, data is collected to understand customer preferences and optimize inventory. Using this data solely for those purposes, rather than for unrelated applications, respects user consent and privacy, aligning with ethical standards.

7. The Role of Regulations and Compliance in Ethical Analytics

Various regulations, such as the GDPR in the EU and the CCPA in California, mandate ethical data practices and protect individual rights. Compliance with these regulations is essential for responsible analytics.

Key Regulatory Considerations

- **GDPR**: Emphasizes user consent, data minimization, and the right to be forgotten, holding companies accountable for protecting personal data.
- **CCPA**: Grants California residents rights over their personal data, including the right to opt-out of data sales and to know how data is used.
- **Industry-Specific Standards**: Some industries, such as healthcare and finance, have additional regulatory standards (e.g., HIPAA in healthcare), governing data handling and ethical practices.

Example of GDPR Compliance in Financial Analytics

Financial institutions must comply with GDPR by ensuring that personal data, such as transaction history and demographic information, is collected with consent and protected from misuse. GDPR also requires financial institutions to delete data upon request, promoting responsible data handling.

8. Implementing Ethical Frameworks and Best Practices

Ethical frameworks provide organizations with guidelines for implementing responsible analytics. These frameworks help ensure that data practices align with societal values and protect individual rights.

Elements of an Ethical Framework

- **Ethics Policies**: Establish clear policies on ethical data use, detailing acceptable and unacceptable practices.
- **Bias Mitigation Plans**: Outline processes for identifying, monitoring, and addressing bias in data and models.

- **Transparency and Accountability Guidelines**: Set standards for transparency and documentation, ensuring stakeholders can understand and question decisions.
- **Ethics Training**: Provide ongoing ethics training for data scientists, analysts, and other team members to ensure they understand ethical standards and practices.

Example: Building an Ethics Framework in E-commerce

An e-commerce company develops an ethics framework covering customer data collection, transparency in product recommendations, and fairness in personalized pricing. This framework promotes ethical practices that enhance customer trust and align with the company's values.

Conclusion

Data ethics and responsible analytics are foundational to creating trustworthy, fair, and transparent AI and data-driven solutions. By adopting principles like privacy protection, bias mitigation, transparency, and accountability, organizations can protect individual rights and ensure that their analytics practices benefit society. As data analytics and AI technologies continue to advance, ethical considerations will be essential for fostering public trust, promoting fairness, and driving innovation responsibly. Developing a strong ethical framework allows organizations to uphold these principles and responsibly navigate the complexities of data analytics.

Strategies for Ensuring Privacy, Fairness, and Transparency in Analytics Projects

With the growing role of data analytics in decision-making, it's essential to implement strategies that protect user privacy, ensure fairness, and maintain transparency. These strategies not only align with ethical standards but also help organizations build trust with users and meet regulatory requirements. This chapter outlines practical strategies for embedding privacy, fairness, and transparency into analytics projects, ensuring responsible and ethical data use.

1. Ensuring Privacy in Analytics Projects

Protecting privacy is a fundamental aspect of responsible analytics. Safeguarding individuals' personal data reduces the risk of misuse, builds trust, and ensures compliance with privacy regulations. Effective privacy strategies encompass informed consent, data minimization, and secure handling of sensitive information.

Key Privacy Strategies

- **Informed Consent and Data Transparency**: Users should know how their data will be collected, processed, and used, and have the ability to consent or opt out.
  - o **Implementation**: Provide clear and accessible privacy policies detailing data collection and usage. Include explanations of how data will be used, and give users options to manage their data preferences.
  - o **Example**: In an app collecting location data, users should see a prompt explaining why their

location is needed (e.g., personalized recommendations) and be able to opt out if desired.

- **Data Minimization**: Collect only the data necessary for analysis, reducing exposure of sensitive information and limiting the risk of misuse.
  - o **Implementation**: Define specific project objectives and collect only data directly relevant to those goals. Avoid collecting excessive information that may not be essential for the analysis.
  - o **Example**: In a customer segmentation analysis, collect basic demographic and purchase data instead of including unnecessary personal details, like home addresses.
- **Anonymization and Pseudonymization**: Remove identifiable information from datasets to protect user identities, especially when sharing data with third parties or using it in analytics.
  - o **Implementation**: Use anonymization techniques to completely strip data of identifiers, or pseudonymization to replace identifiers with anonymous tags, retaining the ability to re-identify individuals if necessary.
  - o **Example**: In a healthcare project analyzing patient data, replace personal identifiers with randomized codes to protect patient privacy while allowing researchers to analyze trends.

- **Implement Data Retention Policies**: Retain data only as long as necessary and securely dispose of it afterward, limiting potential risks if data is breached or mishandled.
  - o **Implementation**: Set clear retention periods based on regulatory guidelines and project requirements. Automate data deletion processes to prevent unnecessary storage.
  - o **Example**: In marketing analytics, retain data for a limited period (e.g., one year) to analyze seasonal trends, then securely delete it to minimize privacy risks.

2. Promoting Fairness in Analytics

Fairness in analytics involves treating all groups equitably, avoiding biases that could lead to unfair treatment, and implementing processes to ensure balanced model outcomes. Unchecked bias can result in discriminatory outcomes, so promoting fairness is essential for ethical analytics, especially in sensitive applications like hiring, lending, and healthcare.

Key Fairness Strategies

- **Balanced Data Collection**: Ensure datasets represent diverse groups and avoid over-representing or under-representing certain demographics, as this can introduce bias into model outcomes.
  - o **Implementation**: Analyze datasets to identify potential imbalances and actively seek out additional data to fill gaps. If certain groups are

underrepresented, consider synthetic data generation to balance the dataset.

- o **Example**: In a hiring algorithm, ensure the dataset includes a balanced representation of applicants from various demographics to avoid bias toward majority groups.
- **Fairness-Aware Model Training**: Use fairness metrics and constraints during model training to ensure that the model does not favor one group over another.
  - o **Implementation**: Integrate fairness metrics such as demographic parity, equal opportunity, and equalized odds into the model training process. Adjust model parameters to achieve balanced outcomes.
  - o **Example**: In credit scoring, adjust the model to ensure that approval rates for applicants from different demographics are comparable, addressing any significant disparities.
- **Bias Audits and Fairness Testing**: Regularly audit models for fairness by examining their impact on different groups and running fairness tests to identify any unintended biases.
  - o **Implementation**: Conduct pre- and post-deployment bias audits. Track fairness metrics over time to monitor if biases emerge or worsen as the model is used.
  - o **Example**: In a health insurance pricing model, conduct regular fairness testing to ensure pricing

does not unfairly penalize any demographic group, such as gender or age groups.

- **Adjust for Historical Biases in Data**: Recognize and address biases in historical data that could carry over into the model, particularly if the data reflects biased decisions made in the past.
    - o **Implementation**: Analyze historical data for known biases, such as biased hiring or lending practices, and adjust weights or use debiasing techniques to counteract them.
    - o **Example**: In a criminal justice model predicting recidivism, adjust for historical biases that may unfairly target certain groups by modifying data weights or excluding biased features.

3. Increasing Transparency in Analytics Projects

Transparency builds trust and understanding by clarifying how data is used, how models make decisions, and how those decisions impact users. Transparency is particularly important in high-stakes applications where users have a vested interest in understanding the basis of model predictions.

Key Transparency Strategies

- **Model Explainability**: Make models interpretable so that users and stakeholders can understand the factors that drive predictions. This is essential for building trust, particularly with complex models.
    - o **Implementation**: Use model-agnostic tools like SHAP (SHapley Additive exPlanations) and LIME (Local Interpretable Model-Agnostic

Explanations) to interpret and explain individual predictions.

- o **Example**: In a loan approval model, use SHAP values to highlight which factors (e.g., income, credit score, loan amount) contributed most to a specific approval or denial decision.

- **Clear Documentation and Disclosure**: Document how data is collected, processed, and used in the model. Disclose any assumptions, limitations, or known biases of the model.

  - o **Implementation**: Provide clear documentation on data sources, preprocessing steps, model design choices, and assumptions. Share this documentation with stakeholders and users where possible.

  - o **Example**: In a predictive policing model, include documentation detailing data sources, such as crime reports, and outline any limitations, such as possible data bias.

- **Interactive Transparency Tools**: Offer tools that allow users to interact with and better understand model predictions. This may include visualizations, feature importance graphs, or interactive dashboards.

  - o **Implementation**: Develop dashboards or visualizations to help stakeholders explore model predictions, see how different factors influence decisions, and understand model confidence.

- **Example**: In a healthcare diagnosis model, provide an interactive tool for doctors to explore how changes in patient features (e.g., age, symptoms) affect the diagnosis prediction, enabling informed decision-making.

- **Engage Stakeholders in the Model Development Process**: Involve stakeholders early on, gathering feedback on model objectives, ethical concerns, and transparency needs. This helps ensure that the model aligns with user expectations and ethical standards.

  - **Implementation**: Conduct workshops or interviews with stakeholders to gather input on the model's design, transparency requirements, and potential impact.

  - **Example**: In a hiring model, involve HR personnel and diversity officers to gather feedback on the model's fairness, ensuring it aligns with the organization's diversity and inclusion goals.

4. Implementing Governance and Accountability Structures

Accountability ensures that data practices are held to high ethical standards and that organizations are responsible for any impact resulting from their analytics projects. Establishing clear governance structures helps maintain ethical standards, ensuring models align with organizational values and user expectations.

Key Accountability Strategies

- **Ethics Committees or Review Boards**: Create ethics committees to review analytics projects, assess ethical risks, and ensure alignment with data ethics standards.
  - ○ **Implementation**: Form a multidisciplinary ethics board, including data scientists, legal experts, and representatives from impacted groups. Regularly review projects and provide feedback.
  - ○ **Example**: In a university using AI to analyze student performance, an ethics board reviews the model to ensure that it supports student growth without unfairly penalizing any group.
- **Model Monitoring and Auditing**: Continuously monitor model performance, fairness, and compliance with ethical standards, especially for models in dynamic environments.
  - ○ **Implementation**: Set up periodic audits of model predictions, tracking fairness, accuracy, and impact metrics. Adjust the model if issues are identified.
  - ○ **Example**: In an insurance pricing model, conduct quarterly audits to ensure pricing fairness and compliance with regulations, making adjustments if certain groups are found to be unfairly impacted.
- **Human-in-the-Loop Oversight**: Include human oversight in the decision-making process, particularly in high-stakes applications like hiring, lending, and

healthcare, where automated decisions should be subject to human review.

- o **Implementation**: Create a system where humans review or override algorithmic decisions as needed, particularly in sensitive cases that may affect individuals' livelihoods or health.
- o **Example**: In a recruitment system using AI to screen applications, allow recruiters to review AI recommendations, ensuring fairness and human oversight in hiring decisions.

- **Accountability Reporting**: Regularly report on the ethical and societal impact of analytics projects to foster transparency and accountability.
  - o **Implementation**: Create public reports summarizing model performance, fairness, compliance, and any significant adjustments made to address ethical concerns.
  - o **Example**: A retail company using AI for personalized marketing could publish an annual accountability report detailing how they protect customer privacy, maintain data security, and avoid discrimination.

Conclusion

Implementing strategies to ensure privacy, fairness, and transparency in analytics projects is essential for ethical, responsible data use. Privacy measures protect individuals' rights and data, fairness initiatives prevent biased outcomes, and transparency fosters trust by making data practices understandable and accountable. Establishing governance and accountability structures further strengthens responsible analytics, ensuring that organizations remain aligned with ethical standards and respond effectively to evolving expectations around data use. By embedding these strategies, data practitioners can make ethical considerations a core part of every analytics project, benefiting users, stakeholders, and society at large.

Best Practices for Building Trust with Stakeholders Through Responsible Data Handling

Trust is fundamental to the success of any analytics project, as stakeholders need to feel confident that their data is used responsibly, securely, and ethically. Building and maintaining this trust requires implementing best practices for data handling that emphasize transparency, accountability, privacy, and fairness. In this chapter, we explore practical ways to build trust with stakeholders through responsible data practices.

1. Prioritizing Transparency in Data Practices

Transparency is essential for earning and keeping stakeholder trust. By being clear and open about data collection, use, and decision-making processes, organizations can build trust with stakeholders who rely on their analytics for insights and decision-making.

Key Strategies for Transparency

- **Communicate Data Collection and Usage Policies**: Ensure stakeholders understand how and why their data is collected and used. Provide clear documentation detailing data collection methods, data sources, and intended uses.

- o **Example**: A fitness app that collects health data could include a user-friendly privacy policy that explains why each type of data is collected (e.g., heart rate for tracking fitness progress) and how it will be used.

- **Provide Access to Model Explanations**: Make sure stakeholders can understand the factors driving model predictions, especially for high-stakes decisions in healthcare, finance, or hiring.

  - o **Example**: In a credit scoring model, share information on factors that affect credit scores (e.g., payment history, credit utilization) so customers understand the criteria influencing their scores.

- **Offer Interactive Dashboards and Reports**: Allow stakeholders to interact with data visualizations, explore model outputs, and gain insights into analytics processes. Interactive tools help stakeholders understand results, building confidence in the analysis.

  - o **Example**: A retail analytics dashboard could display visualizations of sales trends, allowing store managers to interact with the data, view predictions, and better plan inventory.

Benefits: Transparency in data practices fosters stakeholder understanding, reduces the risk of misunderstandings, and creates an environment where users feel comfortable sharing their data.

2. Ensuring Privacy and Data Security

Stakeholders need assurance that their data is handled securely and kept private. Robust data security and privacy practices protect against data breaches, unauthorized access, and misuse, which are essential for building trust.

Key Privacy and Security Practices

- **Implement Strong Data Encryption**: Use encryption to protect data at rest and in transit, ensuring that sensitive information remains secure.
  - Example: In financial analytics, encrypt customer transaction data both in databases and during transmission, protecting it from unauthorized access.
- **Adopt Access Controls and Role-Based Permissions**: Limit data access to only those team members who need it for their work. This minimizes the risk of data misuse and improves accountability.
  - Example: In healthcare, restrict access to patient data so that only authorized personnel, such as doctors and nurses, can view sensitive health information.
- **Anonymize and Aggregate Data Where Possible**: Use anonymization techniques to strip personally identifiable information (PII) from datasets, especially when analyzing or sharing data externally.

- o **Example**: In marketing analytics, anonymize customer data before sharing it with third-party advertisers, ensuring individual identities are protected.
- **Regular Security Audits and Compliance Checks**: Conduct frequent audits of data handling practices to identify vulnerabilities and ensure compliance with privacy regulations like GDPR and CCPA.
    - o **Example**: In an e-commerce platform, schedule annual data security audits to verify adherence to regulatory requirements and ensure the security of customer payment information.

Benefits: Effective data security and privacy practices protect against breaches and foster stakeholder confidence, assuring them that their data is safe and responsibly managed.

3. Promoting Fairness and Addressing Bias

Fairness is a cornerstone of ethical data handling. Stakeholders expect that data analytics and AI models will treat individuals and groups equitably. Ensuring fairness in analytics involves detecting and correcting biases that could result in unfair treatment.

Key Practices for Fairness

- **Conduct Regular Bias Audits**: Evaluate data and model outputs regularly for biases, particularly for high-impact applications like hiring, lending, or medical diagnostics.
    - o **Example**: In a hiring model, conduct periodic bias audits to ensure that the model does not discriminate based on gender, age, or ethnicity.

- **Use Fairness Metrics and Adjust for Bias**: Incorporate fairness metrics into model evaluation to monitor the treatment of different demographic groups. Make adjustments as needed to achieve balanced outcomes.
  - **Example**: In a loan approval model, check metrics like demographic parity to ensure that approval rates are equitable across racial or socioeconomic groups.
- **Diverse Data Collection and Feature Selection**: Ensure that datasets represent diverse populations and that selected features do not introduce discriminatory effects.
  - **Example**: In healthcare, use diverse demographic data to train models for disease prediction, reducing the risk of biased recommendations for underrepresented groups.

Benefits: Fair and unbiased models contribute to equitable treatment, helping organizations maintain credibility and ethical standards. Stakeholders feel assured that analytics will provide fair and accurate insights.

4. Fostering Accountability in Analytics

Accountability in data handling builds trust by assuring stakeholders that an organization is responsible for the outcomes of its analytics processes. Clear accountability practices ensure that data scientists, analysts, and management take ownership of data handling, model performance, and ethical considerations.

Key Accountability Strategies

- **Document Analytics Processes**: Maintain thorough documentation of data collection, preprocessing, modeling, and evaluation processes. This documentation serves as a record that can be reviewed if questions or concerns arise.
  - ○ **Example**: In a retail analytics project, document how sales data is collected, cleaned, and used for forecasting, ensuring transparency about each step in the process.
- **Human Oversight in Critical Decisions**: Implement human-in-the-loop systems for high-stakes applications, ensuring that model outputs are reviewed and validated by qualified personnel.
  - ○ **Example**: In a medical diagnostic model, require a healthcare professional to review AI-generated diagnoses, ensuring that human expertise guides final patient recommendations.
- **Establish Clear Accountability for Model Outcomes**: Assign accountability to specific individuals or teams for monitoring model performance, addressing potential biases, and managing ethical risks.
  - ○ **Example**: In a credit scoring model, assign a data governance team to monitor accuracy, fairness, and compliance, ensuring accountability for the model's outcomes.
- **Stakeholder Engagement and Feedback Mechanisms**: Involve stakeholders in the model development process, seeking feedback on data use,

ethical considerations, and model behavior. Regular feedback builds trust and fosters collaboration.

- o **Example**: In customer analytics, create surveys or forums where customers can voice concerns about data use and provide feedback on how insights are used to personalize marketing.

Benefits: Accountability practices establish clear ownership of data processes, providing stakeholders with confidence that their data is used responsibly and that ethical standards are upheld.

5. Implementing Ethical Frameworks and Governance Policies

Ethical frameworks and governance policies create a structured approach to managing data responsibly, ensuring that ethical standards are consistently applied across analytics projects. This helps organizations make ethical data decisions and fosters trust among stakeholders.

Key Ethical Frameworks and Policies

- **Develop and Communicate an Ethics Charter**: Create an ethics charter outlining the organization's values, principles, and commitments to ethical data practices. Share this charter with stakeholders to clarify the organization's dedication to ethical standards.
  - o **Example**: In an AI-driven customer service system, develop a charter that emphasizes transparency, privacy, and respect for customer data, ensuring ethical data use aligns with corporate values.

- **Establish Data Governance Policies**: Implement data governance policies that specify how data is collected, stored, processed, and shared, including compliance with regulations.
    - **Example**: In healthcare analytics, establish strict governance policies that control access to patient records, ensuring compliance with HIPAA and protecting patient confidentiality.
- **Create an Ethics Committee**: Form an ethics committee to review analytics projects, evaluate ethical risks, and approve models that align with responsible practices.
    - **Example**: In a financial institution, set up an ethics committee that reviews loan approval algorithms for fairness and compliance with anti-discrimination laws.
- **Regular Ethics and Compliance Training**: Provide ongoing ethics training for data scientists, analysts, and other team members to ensure they understand ethical standards, compliance requirements, and best practices.
    - **Example**: In a retail company, conduct quarterly training on data ethics, focusing on responsible handling of customer data and awareness of data protection laws.

Benefits: Ethical frameworks and governance policies establish a culture of responsibility, guiding teams to uphold high ethical standards and building trust with stakeholders by demonstrating a commitment to ethical practices.

6. Communicating Ethical Practices with Stakeholders

Clear communication about ethical practices in data handling is essential for building trust. Stakeholders need to know that ethical considerations are integrated into the organization's analytics processes and that data handling aligns with their values and expectations.

Effective Communication Strategies

- **Publish Transparency and Ethics Reports**: Provide stakeholders with regular reports detailing data usage, model performance, and efforts to ensure privacy, fairness, and transparency.
    - Example: In an e-commerce platform, publish an annual ethics report outlining customer data protection measures, transparency efforts, and model fairness assessments.
- **Host Open Forums or Webinars**: Create opportunities for stakeholders to ask questions and discuss ethical data practices. These forums demonstrate a commitment to accountability and foster open communication.
    - Example: In healthcare, host webinars for patients to explain how their data is used in predictive analytics and answer any privacy or security questions they may have.
- **Develop a Code of Conduct for Data Handling**: Outline a code of conduct that guides how data is handled responsibly, emphasizing privacy, fairness, and ethical considerations.

- Example: A financial institution could adopt a code of conduct for data analysts, specifying respectful and responsible treatment of sensitive customer information in analytics projects.

Benefits: Transparent communication about data handling practices reassures stakeholders that ethical standards are prioritized, building a foundation of trust that can strengthen stakeholder relationships over time.

Conclusion

Building trust with stakeholders requires implementing and communicating responsible data handling practices. Transparency, privacy, fairness, and accountability are the cornerstones of ethical data use, enabling organizations to foster trust through clear and responsible practices. Ethical frameworks and regular communication ensure that stakeholders understand how data is handled and that their values are reflected in analytics projects. By embedding these best practices into data workflows, organizations can establish and maintain strong, trustworthy relationships with stakeholders, setting a high standard for responsible data analytics.

Chapter 10: From Insights to Impact: Presenting Data-Driven Solutions

Techniques for Translating Complex Analytics into Actionable Insights

Data-driven insights are only valuable if they can be clearly communicated and lead to informed decisions. The ability to distill complex analytics into actionable insights is essential for maximizing the impact of data projects. This chapter explores techniques for translating analytics into clear, meaningful recommendations that drive strategic action, emphasizing storytelling, visualization, and effective communication.

1. Crafting a Data Narrative: Telling the Story Behind the Numbers

Data narratives transform raw data into a compelling story, helping stakeholders understand the insights and their implications. A well-crafted narrative places data in a relatable context, connecting insights to business goals and showing stakeholders why these insights matter.

Key Techniques for Building a Data Narrative

- **Define the Central Message**: Identify the core takeaway from your analysis—whether it's an emerging trend, a critical risk, or a new opportunity—and build the narrative around this main insight.
    - **Example**: In a customer retention analysis, the central message could be, "Customer churn is most influenced by subscription costs and lack of loyalty programs."

- **Use a Structured Story Flow**: Structure your story using a familiar framework (e.g., problem, solution, impact) to guide stakeholders through the analysis logically.
  - o **Example**: For a supply chain optimization project, start by defining the current problem (e.g., delays and inefficiencies), introduce the solution (e.g., predictive analytics for demand planning), and highlight the expected impact (e.g., reduced costs and improved fulfillment rates).
- **Include Real-World Examples and Context**: Connect data points to real-world scenarios, using anecdotes, case studies, or hypothetical examples to show how the insights apply to business situations.
  - o **Example**: In a retail sales analysis, illustrate how regional sales trends vary by linking them to specific promotional campaigns or local events that influenced sales performance.

Benefits: A strong data narrative makes complex analytics accessible, aligns stakeholders with the analysis, and provides a clear direction for action.

2. Visualizing Data Effectively: Choosing the Right Charts and Visuals

Visuals are essential for presenting complex data in a digestible format. Choosing the right type of visualization helps communicate insights effectively, enabling stakeholders to grasp patterns, trends, and relationships at a glance.

Guidelines for Effective Data Visualization

- **Match Visuals to Insights**: Use specific chart types to highlight different insights. Line charts are great for trends, bar charts for comparisons, scatter plots for correlations, and heatmaps for geographical data.
  - **Example**: In a sales forecast presentation, use a line chart to show monthly trends and a heatmap to display sales by region.
- **Focus on Clarity and Simplicity**: Avoid clutter and keep visuals clean, emphasizing essential data points and removing unnecessary labels, colors, or gridlines.
  - **Example**: For a customer segmentation analysis, use a simple bar chart to compare average spending across segments, highlighting only the relevant segment differences.
- **Use Colors and Annotations to Draw Attention**: Color can highlight critical information, and annotations can provide explanations directly within visuals, helping stakeholders quickly identify key takeaways.
  - **Example**: In a risk assessment report, use red to indicate high-risk areas on a heatmap and annotate them with the potential impact on business operations.
- **Choose Visuals That Match Stakeholders' Needs**: Tailor visuals to the audience's familiarity with data. Executives may prefer high-level visuals (e.g., dashboards or summary charts), while analysts may appreciate more detailed charts and plots.

○ **Example**: In a financial performance report, create an executive summary with high-level KPIs for leadership and a detailed breakdown for financial analysts.

Benefits: Effective data visualization brings clarity to complex data, enhancing stakeholder understanding and facilitating informed decision-making.

3. Using Dashboards for Real-Time and Ongoing Insights

Dashboards are powerful tools for delivering insights in real-time and providing ongoing access to key metrics. When designed thoughtfully, dashboards allow stakeholders to explore data interactively and gain quick access to critical information.

Dashboard Design Best Practices

- **Prioritize Key Metrics and KPIs**: Choose metrics that align with business goals and focus on KPIs that reflect performance, progress, or risks.
  - ○ **Example**: In a marketing dashboard, prioritize KPIs like customer acquisition cost, conversion rate, and lifetime value to monitor campaign performance.
- **Organize Information Intuitively**: Group related metrics and design the layout to follow a logical flow, making it easy for users to find relevant information.
  - ○ **Example**: For a sales dashboard, place overall revenue metrics at the top, followed by breakdowns by product, region, and sales team performance.

- **Incorporate Drill-Down and Filtering Options**: Enable users to filter data by dimensions (e.g., time period, location) or drill down into specific segments to uncover detailed insights.
  - ○ **Example**: In an HR analytics dashboard, allow users to filter employee metrics by department, location, or tenure to analyze workforce trends.
- **Provide Alerts and Notifications for Key Changes**: Set up automated alerts for significant metric changes, enabling stakeholders to respond promptly to potential risks or opportunities.
  - ○ **Example**: In a financial dashboard, configure alerts to notify finance teams when expenses exceed budget thresholds or revenue falls below targets.

Benefits: Dashboards offer a user-friendly interface for continuous monitoring, enabling stakeholders to track real-time performance, identify emerging trends, and make timely decisions.

4. Communicating Uncertainty and Confidence Levels

Communicating uncertainty is essential in data analysis, as forecasts and predictions inherently involve a level of risk. Clearly expressing uncertainty helps stakeholders make informed decisions and sets realistic expectations for the outcomes of data-driven strategies.

Techniques for Communicating Uncertainty

- **Include Confidence Intervals and Prediction Ranges**: Show the range within which outcomes are likely to fall, providing a visual representation of uncertainty.
  - o **Example**: In a sales forecast report, include a prediction range (e.g., 95% confidence interval) to show potential variability in forecasted figures.
- **Use Probabilistic Language**: Describe outcomes in terms of probabilities to clarify likelihoods, using terms like "likely," "possible," or "unlikely" to describe events.
  - o **Example**: In a risk analysis, say "There's a 70% likelihood of an increase in costs due to supply chain delays," instead of presenting a single cost estimate.
- **Visualize Uncertainty with Shaded Areas or Error Bars**: Use shaded areas in line charts or error bars in bar charts to represent uncertainty, helping stakeholders understand the range of possible outcomes.
  - o **Example**: In a climate forecast, use shaded areas around projected temperature lines to illustrate the range of potential temperature variations.
- **Explain Limitations and Assumptions**: Be transparent about model assumptions, data limitations, and factors that could impact the accuracy of predictions.
  - o **Example**: In a market trend analysis, disclose assumptions about economic growth rates and

customer behavior, explaining how deviations could affect results.

Benefits: Communicating uncertainty builds credibility by setting realistic expectations and providing a complete picture, empowering stakeholders to make well-informed decisions.

5. Providing Actionable Recommendations Based on Insights

Data-driven insights should ultimately lead to clear, actionable recommendations that stakeholders can implement. Transforming analytics into specific actions requires connecting findings to tangible business opportunities or process improvements.

Steps for Delivering Actionable Recommendations

- **Prioritize Findings by Business Impact**: Focus on the insights that have the most significant potential to improve performance, reduce costs, or mitigate risks.
  - **Example**: In an inventory management report, highlight recommendations for reducing stock on low-demand items to save storage costs and free up space for high-demand products.
- **Connect Insights to Business Objectives**: Frame recommendations within the context of organizational goals to make them relevant and actionable.
  - **Example**: In a customer segmentation analysis, suggest targeted marketing strategies for high-value segments that align with the company's revenue growth goals.

- **Provide Step-by-Step Implementation Plans**: Outline practical steps for stakeholders to act on insights, including timelines, resources needed, and potential challenges.
  - o **Example**: In a customer retention report, propose a 3-month action plan for launching a loyalty program, specifying target metrics and steps for implementation.
- **Quantify Expected Outcomes Where Possible**: Estimate potential impact in terms of revenue, cost savings, or efficiency gains, providing stakeholders with a clear understanding of the benefits.
  - o **Example**: In a process optimization analysis, quantify the time savings from automating a manual task, illustrating how this change could improve productivity.

Benefits: Actionable recommendations bridge the gap between insights and impact, equipping stakeholders with clear steps to act on analytics and drive business improvements.

6. Tailoring Presentations to Stakeholder Needs

Effective communication of data-driven insights requires understanding the unique needs and perspectives of different stakeholders. Tailoring presentations to the audience's knowledge level, priorities, and concerns ensures that insights are relevant and persuasive.

Strategies for Audience-Centric Presentations

- **Identify Stakeholder Goals and Concerns**: Customize presentations to address specific priorities, such as cost efficiency for finance teams or customer experience for marketing teams.

- o **Example**: When presenting to marketing, focus on insights related to customer engagement and conversion rates, while emphasizing cost control and ROI for finance.

- **Use Appropriate Language and Detail Levels**: Avoid jargon and technical details for non-expert audiences, and provide more in-depth analysis for technical teams.
  - o **Example**: For executives, present high-level takeaways and impact summaries; for data scientists, dive into detailed methodologies and model performance.

- **Address Potential Questions and Objections**: Anticipate common questions or concerns and prepare answers to clarify points or address potential reservations.
  - o **Example**: In a customer experience analysis, anticipate questions about data sources and privacy, preparing to explain data collection methods and privacy safeguards.

- **Highlight Relevant Action Items for Each Audience**: Identify actions each stakeholder group can take based on the insights, focusing on recommendations aligned with their responsibilities.
  - o **Example**: In an HR turnover analysis, recommend retention strategies for managers (e.g., employee engagement programs) and

budgeting considerations for finance (e.g., cost of recruitment).

Benefits: Tailoring presentations to audience needs ensures that insights are understandable, relevant, and actionable, maximizing the potential for data-driven impact.

Conclusion

Transforming complex analytics into actionable insights requires a combination of storytelling, effective visualization, and tailored communication. By building a clear data narrative, using targeted visualizations, addressing uncertainty, and providing actionable recommendations, data professionals can empower stakeholders to make informed decisions based on the insights derived from data. Tailoring presentations to specific audiences further enhances understanding and encourages action, ensuring that analytics drive meaningful impact across the organization. With these techniques, data practitioners can bridge the gap between data insights and real-world outcomes, turning information into impactful decisions.

Visualization Best Practices for Storytelling with Data

Effective storytelling with data involves more than presenting charts and graphs—it requires thoughtful design and narrative to highlight key insights and guide stakeholders through a clear, impactful story. Visualizations help translate complex data into understandable, memorable insights that prompt decision-making. In this chapter, we cover best practices for using visualization to tell compelling stories with data.

1. Choose the Right Visualization Type to Match the Story

The choice of visualization is foundational to communicating insights effectively. Each chart type has specific strengths and is suited to different types of data stories, so selecting the right format aligns the visual with the insight you want to convey.

Common Chart Types and Their Uses

- **Line Chart**: Ideal for showing trends over time. Use line charts to illustrate gradual changes, seasonal trends, or historical comparisons.
    - **Example**: Use a line chart to show monthly sales growth over the last year, highlighting seasonal peaks and troughs.
- **Bar Chart**: Effective for comparing quantities across categories. Bar charts are great for discrete comparisons, such as regional sales or customer demographics.
    - **Example**: Use a bar chart to compare annual revenue by product category, helping identify top-performing categories.
- **Pie Chart and Donut Chart**: Best for showing parts of a whole, though they should be used sparingly. They work well when illustrating the distribution of a few components.
    - **Example**: A pie chart showing market share among top competitors, with clear labels on each section for clarity.
- **Scatter Plot**: Useful for showing relationships or correlations between two variables. Scatter plots are

especially helpful in finding clusters or trends in datasets.

- o **Example**: In a marketing analysis, use a scatter plot to show the correlation between advertising spend and conversion rates across campaigns.
- **Heatmap**: Ideal for displaying data density or intensity, often used with geospatial or matrix data. Heatmaps reveal patterns in data concentration.
  - o **Example**: Use a heatmap to show user activity on an e-commerce site by hour and day, identifying peak usage times.

Benefits: Using the right visualization type enhances comprehension by aligning the visual with the insight, making it easier for stakeholders to interpret and remember key findings.

2. Simplify and Declutter Visuals for Clarity

A clear, uncluttered visualization ensures that the audience can focus on the most critical information without distraction. Avoid unnecessary elements that could make the visual complex or difficult to interpret.

Best Practices for Simplification

- **Remove Unnecessary Gridlines and Labels**: Gridlines, borders, and excessive labeling can distract viewers. Keep only the essential elements.
  - o **Example**: In a line chart showing sales trends, remove minor gridlines and extraneous labels to keep the focus on the trend line.

- **Limit Colors to Highlight Key Data**: Use a limited color palette to avoid overwhelming the viewer. Reserve bold or contrasting colors to highlight essential data points or trends.
  - **Example**: In a revenue bar chart, use a single color for most bars and a contrasting color for the top-performing product line.
- **Use Clean Fonts and Legible Sizes**: Choose fonts that are clear and professional, and ensure text sizes are large enough to read easily without overwhelming the visual.
  - **Example**: In a dashboard, use a clear, sans-serif font for all text, with larger sizes for titles and key figures, and smaller sizes for supporting labels.
- **Keep Titles and Axis Labels Descriptive but Concise**: Titles and labels should clearly describe what's being shown, making it easier for viewers to understand the context at a glance.
  - **Example**: Instead of "Revenue," use "Quarterly Revenue (in Millions)" as the chart title to specify the time frame and scale.

Benefits: Simplifying visuals improves readability and ensures that the audience's attention is directed toward the most relevant insights, making the data story clearer and more impactful.

3. Use Color Strategically to Emphasize and Differentiate

Color is a powerful tool for highlighting important information, distinguishing between categories, and reinforcing the data narrative. Using color purposefully can help emphasize key insights and guide viewers through the story.

Best Practices for Using Color

- **Limit Color Usage**: Stick to a maximum of 3-5 colors to keep the visual clean and cohesive, using more intense colors to emphasize key data points.
    - o **Example**: In a customer satisfaction report, use a single color for neutral ratings and different shades to highlight positive and negative ratings.
- **Apply Color to Show Trends or Categories**: Use gradients to illustrate intensity or change over time, and distinct colors to differentiate categories.
    - o **Example**: In a temperature heatmap, apply a gradient from cool blue to warm red to show low to high values, making intensity changes intuitive.
- **Use Consistent Color Schemes Across Visuals**: Choose a standard color scheme for all visualizations within a presentation or dashboard to create a cohesive and professional look.
    - o **Example**: For a quarterly business review, use blue for positive metrics, red for negative metrics, and gray for neutral figures across all visuals.
- **Consider Accessibility and Contrast**: Ensure colors have sufficient contrast to be readable, especially for

color-blind viewers. Use color-blind-friendly palettes and avoid relying on color alone to convey information.

- ○ **Example**: In a profit and loss chart, use patterns or labels in addition to colors to differentiate between gains and losses, accommodating color-blind stakeholders.

Benefits: Strategic color use enhances the impact of key data points, makes complex visuals more digestible, and improves accessibility, allowing the audience to focus on what matters most.

4. Add Context with Annotations and Descriptive Labels

Annotations provide context within the visualization, helping viewers understand the significance of specific data points, trends, or anomalies. Well-placed annotations make it easier for stakeholders to grasp the meaning behind the numbers.

Effective Annotation Practices

- **Highlight Key Data Points**: Add labels or annotations directly on significant data points, such as peaks, troughs, or outliers, to draw attention to critical insights.
  - ○ **Example**: In a sales trend line chart, add a label to indicate the highest sales month, along with a short note on contributing factors (e.g., "Holiday Promotion Boost").
- **Explain Trends or Anomalies**: Use text boxes to clarify unexpected trends or anomalies, providing context for changes in the data.

- o **Example**: In a stock price chart, annotate a sharp decline with an explanation, such as "Market Reaction to New Regulations," to give viewers immediate context.
- **Use Tooltips for Interactive Visuals**: In dashboards, incorporate tooltips that display additional information when users hover over data points, allowing them to explore details without cluttering the visual.
  - o **Example**: In a customer demographics dashboard, add tooltips that show customer count and average spend per demographic group.
- **Avoid Over-Annotation**: Focus annotations on essential insights, avoiding excessive text that could overwhelm the viewer. Select only the most impactful points for annotation.
  - o **Example**: In a cost analysis chart, annotate only the top three cost contributors, rather than every data point, to keep the visual clean.

Benefits: Thoughtful annotations provide essential context, making it easier for viewers to interpret data accurately and reinforcing the narrative with additional information.

5. Use Dynamic and Interactive Elements for Enhanced Engagement

Interactivity can deepen understanding by allowing stakeholders to explore data at their own pace, view specific segments, or drill down into details. Dynamic elements create a more engaging experience, transforming static data into actionable insights.

Best Practices for Interactive Visuals

- **Enable Filters and Drill-Down Options**: Allow viewers to filter by categories or drill down into data for deeper insights, making it easier to analyze specific segments.
  - ○ **Example**: In a sales dashboard, include filters for region and product line, enabling managers to view performance in their specific areas of responsibility.
- **Incorporate Time-Sliders for Temporal Data**: Use time sliders to allow viewers to explore data across different periods, which is particularly helpful for analyzing trends over time.
  - ○ **Example**: In a web traffic analysis dashboard, add a time slider to let users view daily, weekly, or monthly data trends, revealing patterns in user behavior.
- **Use Hover-Over Tooltips**: For crowded visuals, add hover-over tooltips that display details when users interact with specific data points, reducing visual clutter.
  - ○ **Example**: In a budget variance chart, use tooltips to show the percentage variance for each expense category, reducing the need for extensive labels.
- **Add Interactive Annotations for Key Insights**: Provide clickable annotations that reveal more

information or link to related insights, encouraging exploration without cluttering the visual.

- o **Example**: In a customer satisfaction dashboard, add clickable icons over key metrics that reveal the survey questions or specific feedback contributing to the score.

Benefits: Interactive visuals engage stakeholders, allowing them to explore data insights in depth, personalize their analysis, and make better-informed decisions.

6. Tell a Cohesive Story Across Multiple Visuals

When presenting multiple visuals, ensure they work together to build a cohesive narrative. This involves ordering visuals logically, using consistent design elements, and linking insights across charts to guide viewers through the data story.

Techniques for Building a Cohesive Visual Story

- **Order Visuals Logically**: Arrange visuals in a sequence that reflects the narrative structure (e.g., overview, breakdown, recommendations), guiding viewers through the insights.
  - o **Example**: In a marketing report, begin with an overall performance summary, then present visuals on campaign performance, and end with customer behavior insights.
- **Maintain Consistent Design Elements**: Use the same color palette, font style, and chart types across visuals to create a professional and cohesive look.
  - o **Example**: For a company performance dashboard, use the same color scheme for profit-

related metrics across charts, reinforcing consistency.

- **Link Related Insights Across Visuals**: Connect insights across multiple visuals to reinforce key points and provide context for deeper analysis.
  - ○ **Example**: In a product launch report, link a customer engagement chart with a sales growth chart to show how engagement impacted revenue.
- **Summarize Key Takeaways**: End with a summary visualization, such as a KPI dashboard or bullet points, to reinforce the most important insights from the data story.
  - ○ **Example**: After presenting a series of charts on cost-saving initiatives, conclude with a summary dashboard highlighting overall savings and impact metrics.

Benefits: A cohesive visual story ensures that each visualization builds on the previous one, creating a seamless narrative that makes complex insights accessible and memorable.

Conclusion

Visualization best practices are essential for effectively communicating data-driven insights and guiding stakeholders through a compelling story. By selecting the right visualization types, simplifying visuals, using color strategically, adding context with annotations, incorporating interactivity, and building a cohesive narrative, data professionals can transform complex analytics into clear, impactful insights. These techniques ensure that data-driven stories resonate with stakeholders, enabling them to understand key findings and make informed, actionable decisions. With strong visual storytelling, data can drive real impact and facilitate better outcomes across organizations.

Methods for Influencing Decisions and Driving Change with Clear, Persuasive Analytics Presentations

Effectively presenting data-driven insights is key to influencing decisions and driving positive change. A well-crafted analytics presentation doesn't just inform—it persuades, aligning stakeholders around a common understanding and motivating action. This chapter explores methods for structuring and delivering analytics presentations that resonate with stakeholders, helping them make data-informed decisions with confidence.

1. Start with a Strong Executive Summary

The executive summary serves as the anchor of any analytics presentation. A clear, concise summary provides stakeholders with the main takeaways upfront, setting the stage for the detailed insights that follow.

Key Elements of a Strong Executive Summary

- **Highlight Key Findings**: Present the most critical insights right at the beginning, capturing the audience's attention and framing the presentation's purpose.
    - **Example**: For a customer retention analysis, start with "Customer churn is 15% higher in the

last quarter, largely influenced by reduced engagement in the 18-25 age group."

- **Summarize Recommendations**: Briefly state actionable recommendations based on the data insights, giving stakeholders a preview of the proposed actions.
  - ○ **Example**: "To improve retention, we recommend introducing loyalty incentives for younger customers and enhancing personalized engagement."
- **Use a Visual Overview of Key Metrics**: A snapshot of key metrics in a dashboard or infographic format can provide a quick, high-level view.
  - ○ **Example**: In a financial performance report, include a one-slide dashboard with revenue, profit margin, and expense breakdowns.

Benefits: A strong executive summary builds interest, aligns stakeholders on the presentation's purpose, and provides a reference point for the insights to come.

2. Structure the Presentation Around the Audience's Goals

Understanding the goals, interests, and concerns of your audience is critical to delivering an impactful presentation. By focusing on insights that matter most to them, you can create a narrative that directly addresses their needs and drives engagement.

Strategies for Audience-Centric Structuring

- **Identify Key Audience Concerns**: Start by addressing any specific challenges or objectives that stakeholders are focused on.

- o **Example**: When presenting to marketing, focus on customer behavior insights and segmentation, while for finance, highlight metrics like ROI and cost efficiency.
- **Organize Insights by Relevance**: Structure the presentation so that high-priority insights appear first, followed by supporting data and less critical findings.
  - o **Example**: In a product launch analysis, begin with overall launch performance, followed by segment-specific data, such as customer feedback and regional sales.
- **Relate Insights to Business Objectives**: Connect each insight back to the organization's strategic goals, helping stakeholders see the bigger picture.
  - o **Example**: In an employee engagement report, relate survey findings to organizational goals of improving productivity and reducing turnover.

Benefits: A well-structured, audience-focused presentation captures attention, addresses relevant concerns, and increases the likelihood of buy-in from key decision-makers.

3. Use Storytelling to Make Data More Relatable

Storytelling transforms data into a relatable narrative, helping stakeholders connect emotionally with the information and better understand its relevance. A compelling story can illustrate the implications of data-driven insights and motivate stakeholders to take action.

Best Practices for Data Storytelling

- **Introduce the Problem and Context**: Frame the data in terms of a problem or opportunity, making the story relatable and engaging.
  - **Example**: "Our customer retention rates are declining, particularly among younger users. Here's how we can reverse this trend."
- **Use Real-Life Examples or Case Studies**: Incorporate examples or case studies to illustrate how data insights apply to real-world scenarios.
  - **Example**: In a customer satisfaction analysis, highlight a recent case where improved response time led to higher satisfaction scores, linking it to potential improvements.
- **Follow a Clear Narrative Arc**: Structure the story with a beginning (the current situation), middle (the analysis and findings), and end (the recommended actions and expected outcomes).
  - **Example**: "Last quarter, we faced increased costs due to inefficient supply chain management. Here's what the data revealed, and how we can streamline operations."

Benefits: Storytelling engages stakeholders emotionally, making data more memorable and impactful, while helping stakeholders visualize how insights connect to their roles and objectives.

4. Support Insights with Visuals that Reinforce Key Points

Data visuals are powerful tools for communicating insights, but they are most effective when they reinforce the presentation's main message. Well-chosen visuals highlight patterns, simplify complex information, and enhance the clarity of the data story.

Best Practices for Supporting Insights with Visuals

- **Use Highlight Colors to Emphasize Important Data**: Draw attention to critical metrics or trends by using bold colors for key data points, while keeping other data in muted tones.
  - o **Example**: In a budget report, use a bold color to highlight expenses that exceeded the budget, while displaying other expenses in gray.
- **Leverage Comparison Charts for Decision-Making**: Use side-by-side bar charts, before-and-after visuals, or heatmaps to make it easy to compare performance or outcomes.
  - o **Example**: In a product performance review, show a bar chart comparing unit sales across product lines to highlight top and underperforming products.
- **Add Annotations for Key Takeaways**: Label specific data points or trends with short annotations, ensuring stakeholders can quickly interpret the visual's message.
  - o **Example**: In a quarterly sales growth chart, annotate each peak and dip with the factors contributing to changes, such as "Holiday season surge" or "Supply chain delay."

Benefits: Well-designed visuals make data-driven insights more accessible, reinforcing key points and helping stakeholders quickly grasp the information.

5. Use Clear and Persuasive Language to Build Credibility

The language used in an analytics presentation significantly influences how insights are perceived. Clear, persuasive language enhances credibility and builds confidence in the analysis, while overly technical or ambiguous language can detract from the message.

Techniques for Clear and Persuasive Communication

- **Avoid Jargon and Technical Terms**: Use plain language to describe findings, making sure terms are understandable to all stakeholders.
    - **Example**: Instead of "statistically significant," say "a meaningful increase" when describing changes that are important for decision-making.
- **Highlight Certainty and Acknowledge Limitations**: Be transparent about the level of confidence in predictions and any limitations of the data or analysis.
    - **Example**: "We're confident that this trend will continue under current conditions, though changes in market demand could impact results."
- **Use Action-Oriented Phrases**: Frame recommendations with action-oriented language to make next steps clear and actionable.
    - **Example**: "Implement a loyalty program targeting repeat customers to increase retention by 20% over the next quarter."

Benefits: Clear, straightforward language enhances understanding, instills confidence in the findings, and encourages stakeholders to take action on the insights presented.

6. Anticipate Questions and Address Potential Objections

A persuasive presentation proactively addresses stakeholder questions and potential objections, demonstrating thorough analysis and understanding of different perspectives. Preparing for these questions shows credibility and builds trust in the data's accuracy.

Best Practices for Addressing Questions and Objections

- **Present Assumptions and Methodology Transparently**: Explain the assumptions, data sources, and methods used in the analysis, providing context for the insights.
  - o **Example**: In a sales forecast, clarify that projections assume a stable economy and consistent product demand.
- **Anticipate and Prepare Responses to Common Objections**: Consider likely questions or pushbacks from stakeholders and prepare responses backed by data or additional context.
  - o **Example**: In a budget allocation analysis, be prepared to justify higher spending recommendations with evidence of expected ROI.
- **Include Backup Slides with Supporting Data**: Have extra slides with detailed data, charts, or technical information ready to address specific questions without overwhelming the main presentation.

- Example: For a staffing analysis, prepare a backup slide showing productivity metrics by department to explain recommended hiring increases.

Benefits: Anticipating questions and objections demonstrates thorough preparation, reduces the risk of misunderstandings, and strengthens stakeholder confidence in the analysis.

7. Conclude with a Compelling Call to Action

A strong call to action provides clear next steps and motivates stakeholders to act on the insights presented. This final step reinforces the presentation's message and ensures that insights translate into impactful decisions.

Key Elements of a Compelling Call to Action

- **Summarize Key Takeaways and Impact**: Recap the most critical insights and the anticipated impact of following the recommendations.
  - Example: "By implementing the proposed customer engagement initiatives, we can reduce churn by 15%, adding an estimated $1M in annual revenue."
- **Outline Specific Action Steps**: Provide a clear list of next steps, specifying who should act, what actions are needed, and when they should be completed.
  - Example: "1) Launch targeted campaigns for high-risk customers by next month; 2) Introduce loyalty incentives within Q3."

- **Quantify the Benefits**: Where possible, include concrete metrics or estimates that demonstrate the value of taking action on the insights.
  - **Example**: "Implementing automation in the billing process will save an estimated 500 work hours annually, reducing operational costs by 10%."
- **Encourage Immediate Follow-Up**: Suggest specific follow-up actions or meetings to review progress, ensuring momentum and accountability.
  - **Example**: "We recommend a follow-up meeting in two weeks to discuss progress on the loyalty program rollout and adjust strategies as needed."

Benefits: A clear, compelling call to action motivates stakeholders to implement data-driven recommendations, translating insights into concrete, impactful changes.

Conclusion

Presenting data-driven insights effectively requires more than just data—it involves crafting a persuasive narrative, supporting insights with visuals, using clear language, and addressing potential objections. By structuring presentations around stakeholder goals, using storytelling, and ending with a strong call to action, data professionals can drive meaningful change and inspire decision-making based on solid analytics. These techniques ensure that analytics presentations resonate with stakeholders, encourage buy-in, and lead to real-world impact from data insights.

Chapter 11: Future Trends in Data Analytics and Machine Learning

Exploration of Emerging Trends in AI, Including AutoML, Reinforcement Learning, and Generative AI

As data analytics and machine learning continue to advance, new trends and technologies are shaping the future of AI, creating exciting opportunities for automation, efficiency, and innovation. Emerging trends like AutoML, reinforcement learning, and generative AI are driving developments that expand the reach of machine learning and make it accessible to more organizations. This chapter explores these technologies, their applications, and the potential impact on the field of data analytics.

1. AutoML: Automating the Machine Learning Pipeline

AutoML (Automated Machine Learning) simplifies the process of building, selecting, and tuning machine learning models, enabling organizations to create powerful models without requiring extensive expertise in data science. AutoML automates various steps in the machine learning pipeline, including data preprocessing, feature selection, model selection, and hyperparameter tuning.

Key Features of AutoML

- **End-to-End Automation**: AutoML automates the workflow from data preprocessing to model deployment, enabling non-experts to build predictive models with minimal manual intervention.

- **Model Selection and Tuning**: AutoML selects and tunes the best algorithms based on the data, choosing from a range of models (e.g., decision trees, neural networks, ensemble methods) to optimize performance.
- **Explainability and Transparency**: Many AutoML tools include model interpretability features, making it easier to understand model decisions and maintain transparency.

Applications of AutoML

- **Business Forecasting**: AutoML is increasingly used for sales forecasting, demand prediction, and inventory management, providing accurate predictions with limited manual tuning.
- **Customer Segmentation**: AutoML can identify customer segments based on purchasing behavior, demographics, and engagement, allowing businesses to personalize marketing strategies.
- **Healthcare and Diagnostics**: In medical diagnostics, AutoML aids in building models that analyze patient data and predict health outcomes, accelerating the adoption of predictive analytics in healthcare.

Benefits of AutoML

AutoML democratizes machine learning, making it accessible to non-experts and allowing organizations to accelerate the deployment of machine learning models. By automating repetitive tasks, AutoML also frees data scientists to focus on more complex aspects of projects, driving efficiency and innovation.

2. Reinforcement Learning: Learning from Interaction and Feedback

Reinforcement learning (RL) is a type of machine learning where an agent learns to make decisions by interacting with an environment and receiving feedback in the form of rewards or penalties. RL is inspired by behavioral psychology and has applications in areas where decision-making unfolds over time, allowing the model to learn optimal actions to maximize cumulative rewards.

Key Concepts in Reinforcement Learning

- **Agents and Environments**: The agent is the learner or decision-maker, while the environment represents the context or system within which the agent operates.
- **Reward System**: The agent receives rewards (positive or negative) based on actions, guiding it to make decisions that maximize cumulative rewards over time.
- **Exploration vs. Exploitation**: RL involves a balance between exploring new actions to discover rewards and exploiting known actions to maximize rewards.

Applications of Reinforcement Learning

- **Autonomous Vehicles**: RL helps autonomous vehicles learn to navigate, avoid obstacles, and make complex driving decisions, improving safety and efficiency.
- **Robotics**: In robotics, RL enables robots to learn tasks through trial and error, from object manipulation to complex assembly line tasks.
- **Personalized Recommendations**: In streaming services and e-commerce, RL optimizes content

recommendations by learning user preferences and adapting suggestions over time.

- **Dynamic Pricing and Resource Allocation**: RL is used in industries like retail and energy to set prices dynamically based on demand or allocate resources efficiently in real-time environments.

Benefits of Reinforcement Learning

Reinforcement learning allows machines to learn complex, sequential decision-making processes, making it suitable for real-world applications where actions have long-term consequences. Its ability to adapt and improve over time holds promise for fields requiring continual optimization, such as supply chain management, finance, and operations.

3. Generative AI: Creating New Data and Content

Generative AI refers to models that can create new content, such as images, text, audio, or video, based on patterns learned from existing data. These models, particularly generative adversarial networks (GANs) and transformer-based models, have transformed the creative landscape, allowing machines to generate realistic and original content.

Key Techniques in Generative AI

- **Generative Adversarial Networks (GANs)**: GANs use a generator and discriminator in a competitive setting to create highly realistic images, videos, and other content.
- **Transformer Models**: Models like GPT (Generative Pre-trained Transformer) and BERT (Bidirectional Encoder Representations from Transformers) use large amounts

of text data to generate coherent text, answer questions, and engage in conversation.

Applications of Generative AI

- **Content Creation**: Generative AI is used in content creation for marketing, entertainment, and education, including automated article writing, image generation, and video editing.

- **Healthcare and Drug Discovery**: Generative AI models are used to create synthetic molecules or simulate protein structures, aiding drug discovery and medical research.

- **Virtual Assistants and Chatbots**: Generative AI powers advanced conversational agents, allowing them to understand and generate human-like responses in real time.

- **Data Augmentation**: Generative models create synthetic data to augment training datasets, particularly useful for improving model accuracy in scenarios with limited data.

Benefits of Generative AI

Generative AI opens up new possibilities for innovation, particularly in creative industries, healthcare, and AI research. By generating new content and data, it enables businesses to enhance customer experiences, automate repetitive content creation tasks, and develop novel solutions.

4. Edge AI: Bringing AI to the Edge of Networks

Edge AI involves deploying machine learning models on devices at the network's edge (e.g., smartphones, IoT devices) rather than in centralized data centers. This trend addresses the need for real-time processing, reduced latency, and privacy by enabling devices to process data locally without sending it to the cloud.

Key Features of Edge AI

- **Real-Time Processing**: Edge AI performs computations directly on devices, enabling real-time analysis and decision-making.
- **Privacy and Security**: Processing data locally reduces the risk of data breaches and minimizes the need to transmit sensitive information.
- **Reduced Latency**: By processing data on-device, edge AI reduces latency, which is critical for applications requiring immediate feedback.

Applications of Edge AI

- **Smart Cities**: Edge AI supports real-time monitoring of traffic, public safety, and environmental conditions, enabling rapid response to changing conditions.
- **Healthcare and Wearables**: Edge AI enables health monitoring on devices like wearables, where data can be processed in real-time to alert users or medical professionals.
- **Industrial Automation**: In manufacturing, edge AI analyzes sensor data on machinery to detect anomalies and optimize maintenance without relying on remote servers.
- **Augmented Reality and Gaming**: Edge AI powers augmented reality applications and mobile gaming by

delivering seamless experiences without cloud dependencies.

Benefits of Edge AI

Edge AI reduces dependency on cloud infrastructure, increases data privacy, and allows for real-time processing. It is particularly valuable in industries with strict data privacy requirements and applications that demand instant feedback, such as autonomous vehicles, healthcare, and industrial automation.

5. Explainable AI (XAI): Enhancing Transparency and Trust

As machine learning models become more complex, explainable AI (XAI) seeks to make them understandable to humans. XAI addresses the "black box" problem by providing insights into how and why a model makes specific predictions, fostering transparency, accountability, and trust in AI systems.

Key Concepts in Explainable AI

- **Interpretability**: XAI provides tools to explain model outputs, helping users understand which features or variables influenced a decision.
- **Model Transparency**: XAI techniques enhance transparency by making machine learning models, particularly deep learning models, more accessible to non-experts.
- **Feature Attribution**: Tools like SHAP (SHapley Additive exPlanations) and LIME (Local Interpretable Model-Agnostic Explanations) offer feature attribution, showing the influence of individual variables on predictions.

Applications of Explainable AI

- **Healthcare Diagnostics**: XAI helps healthcare professionals understand AI-based diagnostic recommendations, allowing them to validate and trust the model's output.
- **Finance and Credit Scoring**: Explainable AI allows financial institutions to justify credit decisions by clarifying how various factors, like credit history and income, influence approval.
- **Compliance and Regulatory Reporting**: In regulated industries, XAI assists in documenting AI decisions, supporting compliance with laws requiring transparency in automated decision-making.
- **Customer Support and Personalization**: XAI enables businesses to explain personalization recommendations (e.g., content recommendations) to users, increasing trust in automated systems.

Benefits of Explainable AI

Explainable AI improves model transparency and helps build trust with users by clarifying how decisions are made. This is especially important in industries with high-stakes applications like healthcare, finance, and legal, where decisions must be justifiable and understandable.

6. Federated Learning: Collaborative Learning Without Data Sharing

Federated learning is a method that allows machine learning models to be trained across multiple decentralized devices or servers without transferring raw data to a central location. This approach enhances data privacy and security while enabling collaborative learning.

Key Features of Federated Learning

- **Decentralized Training**: Instead of sending data to a central server, federated learning trains models locally on devices and only aggregates model updates.
- **Privacy Preservation**: Since raw data never leaves the local device, federated learning minimizes data exposure and aligns with privacy regulations.
- **Scalability**: Federated learning allows scalable model training across a vast number of devices

Implications of Advancements in Data Analytics and Machine Learning for Professionals

The rapid advancements in data analytics and machine learning are transforming how data professionals work, offering new tools, methodologies, and challenges. Emerging technologies like AutoML, reinforcement learning, generative AI, edge computing, and federated learning present both opportunities and demands, requiring data professionals to adapt and expand their skillsets. This chapter explores the implications of these advancements for data analytics professionals, highlighting the skills, responsibilities, and strategic adjustments needed to stay relevant in a dynamic field.

1. Expanding Skill Sets to Include New Technologies and Techniques

The emergence of advanced technologies such as AutoML, reinforcement learning, and generative AI requires data professionals to continually evolve their skillsets. Mastering these tools enables professionals to leverage new capabilities and gain competitive advantages in their work.

Key Skills in Demand

- **Automation and AutoML**: As AutoML becomes more widely used, professionals need to understand how to leverage these platforms to automate repetitive tasks while maintaining control over model quality and interpretability.

- **Reinforcement Learning and Advanced Algorithms**: Reinforcement learning opens up opportunities in industries like robotics, finance, and logistics, requiring professionals to learn new algorithms and how to apply them in real-world scenarios.

- **Generative AI and Content Creation**: Knowledge of generative models, such as GANs and transformer models, is increasingly valuable for professionals in marketing, media, and design who wish to create data-driven content.

- **Edge and Federated Learning**: Working with edge and federated learning requires familiarity with decentralized data processing, making these skills crucial for industries prioritizing real-time analytics and privacy, like healthcare and IoT.

Implications: The demand for new technical skills encourages data professionals to invest in continuous learning. Those who adapt to and adopt these emerging technologies can bring innovative solutions to their organizations, staying at the forefront of the industry.

2. Embracing Automation to Increase Efficiency and Focus on High-Impact Work

As automation tools like AutoML reduce the time spent on repetitive tasks, data professionals can shift their focus toward more strategic, high-impact work. Automation does not replace the need for human expertise; instead, it augments it, allowing professionals to focus on interpretation, problem-solving, and strategic recommendations.

Shifts in Focus Enabled by Automation

- **Greater Emphasis on Business Problem Definition**: With AutoML handling model selection and hyperparameter tuning, data professionals can dedicate more time to defining the problem, selecting the right data, and ensuring that the analysis aligns with business goals.
- **Enhanced Focus on Interpretation and Communication**: As AutoML simplifies the technical modeling process, professionals need to excel at interpreting results and communicating actionable insights to stakeholders.
- **Model Monitoring and Continuous Improvement**: AutoML and automation make it easy to deploy models but also necessitate ongoing monitoring and adjustments, especially as business conditions or data drift.

Implications: Automation enables data professionals to prioritize higher-value activities, such as understanding business objectives, refining data strategies, and communicating insights. This shift enhances their strategic role in organizations and requires strong business acumen and communication skills.

3. Navigating the Ethical and Responsible Use of AI and Data

The increased complexity and power of machine learning models, such as reinforcement learning and generative AI, raise ethical questions that data professionals must address. As models become more sophisticated, so too do the challenges of ensuring fairness, transparency, and accountability in AI-driven decisions.

New Ethical Considerations

- **Explainability and Transparency**: Advanced models, particularly deep learning and generative models, often operate as "black boxes." Data professionals must advocate for explainable AI, using tools like SHAP and LIME to make models understandable to stakeholders.

- **Bias and Fairness**: As machine learning models increasingly impact hiring, lending, and healthcare, it is crucial to identify and mitigate bias. Professionals are responsible for assessing model fairness and ensuring that predictions do not reinforce harmful stereotypes.

- **Privacy and Data Security in Federated Learning**: Federated learning and edge AI offer new opportunities to protect data privacy by keeping data decentralized.

Data professionals must implement these models responsibly, safeguarding privacy while balancing analytical needs.

Implications: Data professionals will increasingly serve as stewards of ethical AI, responsible for maintaining fairness, transparency, and accountability. This role requires awareness of ethical frameworks, proficiency with interpretability tools, and a commitment to ongoing ethical training.

4. Adapting to Real-Time and Decentralized Analytics

Technologies like edge AI and federated learning push analytics beyond centralized data centers, requiring data professionals to adapt to real-time, decentralized data processing. In fields like healthcare, IoT, and autonomous systems, real-time decision-making has become essential, creating demand for skills in decentralized data processing and edge computing.

New Responsibilities with Decentralized Analytics

- **Understanding Edge Computing and Real-Time Data Processing**: Data professionals working with IoT or real-time applications must learn to handle data on distributed networks, enabling low-latency processing and fast responses.

- **Managing Data Privacy and Security in Distributed Environments**: Decentralized analytics demand strong data governance skills, as sensitive data is increasingly stored and processed across numerous devices.

- **Maintaining Data Quality Across Devices**: Professionals must address challenges in ensuring data consistency, accuracy, and quality across decentralized systems where data may be fragmented or noisy.

Implications: The shift toward real-time, decentralized analytics requires data professionals to develop skills in edge computing, data security, and quality control in distributed networks. This trend emphasizes the need for adaptability as data processing becomes more fragmented and immediate.

5. Enhancing Collaboration with Business Units through AI-Driven Insights

As advanced analytics become more integrated into business processes, data professionals are expected to work closely with non-technical departments, translating complex models into actionable insights. The role of data professionals as strategic partners to business units becomes more critical, and they must bridge the gap between technical insights and business strategy.

Key Collaboration Strategies

- **Communicating Data Insights to Non-Technical Teams**: Professionals must explain insights from complex models in simple terms, showing how data-driven insights align with business goals and operational needs.
- **Building User-Friendly Dashboards and Tools**: Creating interactive dashboards with AutoML and visualization tools allows non-technical stakeholders to explore data insights independently, enhancing engagement.

- **Providing Training and Support for AI Applications**: As AI-driven tools are deployed, data professionals may be called upon to train business users, ensuring they understand and trust automated recommendations.

Implications: As data professionals become increasingly embedded within business units, communication skills and the ability to translate insights for a non-technical audience are paramount. Success in this role requires building strong relationships, aligning analytics with organizational goals, and promoting a culture of data-driven decision-making.

6. Developing Specialized Expertise for High-Demand Applications

With the growing number of machine learning applications, specialization is becoming increasingly valuable in areas like healthcare analytics, autonomous systems, and natural language processing (NLP). By focusing on high-demand, domain-specific applications, data professionals can deepen their expertise and position themselves as valuable assets within their industries.

Areas of Specialized Expertise

- **Healthcare and Diagnostics**: Specialized knowledge in medical data analysis, federated learning for patient privacy, and explainable AI are critical in healthcare applications.
- **Autonomous Systems and Robotics**: Understanding reinforcement learning, real-time processing, and ethical considerations is essential for professionals working in autonomous systems.

- **Natural Language Processing (NLP)**: With generative AI transforming language models, NLP expertise is in demand for applications like chatbots, virtual assistants, and sentiment analysis.
- **Financial Analytics**: Expertise in XAI and reinforcement learning helps professionals address the complex decision-making needs of the finance sector, from credit scoring to fraud detection.

Implications: Developing specialized knowledge within a high-demand application area enables data professionals to create targeted, impactful solutions. Specialization enhances career prospects and allows professionals to drive innovation in their chosen fields.

7. Embracing Continuous Learning and Adaptation

With AI and machine learning technologies evolving rapidly, continuous learning is crucial for data professionals. To stay relevant, data professionals need to adapt to new tools, methodologies, and industry standards, ensuring they remain capable of leveraging cutting-edge advancements effectively.

Strategies for Continuous Learning

- **Enroll in Specialized Training and Certification Programs**: Courses on new technologies, such as AutoML, reinforcement learning, or edge AI, provide structured learning opportunities to master emerging skills.
- **Engage with the Data Science Community**: Participating in conferences, online forums, and

communities allows professionals to stay informed about new trends, best practices, and tools.

- **Experiment with New Technologies**: Hands-on experimentation with new tools and platforms enables professionals to develop practical skills, staying agile as new solutions emerge.
- **Follow Industry Leaders and Research**: Keeping up with thought leaders, academic research, and industry publications provides insights into the future direction of data science and machine learning.

Implications: A commitment to continuous learning ensures that data professionals remain competitive and informed, able to harness the latest advancements in AI. Those who embrace adaptability and lifelong learning will be best positioned to drive innovation and create impact in a rapidly changing field.

Conclusion

Advancements in data analytics and machine learning are reshaping the responsibilities and skill requirements for data professionals. As AutoML, reinforcement learning, generative AI, edge computing, and other trends reshape the landscape, data professionals must adapt by expanding their technical skills, focusing on ethical considerations, and collaborating closely with business units. By embracing continuous learning, developing specialized expertise, and adopting a proactive approach to emerging technologies, data professionals can drive innovation and maintain their value in a dynamic field. The future of data analytics holds vast potential for those who are prepared to evolve and lead in a rapidly advancing digital world.

Preparation Tips for Staying Relevant and Leveraging New Technologies in Analytics

In an era of rapid technological change, data analytics professionals need to continually evolve to stay relevant and effectively leverage new technologies. Emerging fields like AutoML, reinforcement learning, edge AI, and generative AI demand updated skills, adaptive mindsets, and a commitment to lifelong learning. This chapter provides practical tips for preparing to work with these advancements, empowering data professionals to navigate an ever-evolving landscape.

1. Build a Strong Foundation in Core Data Skills

A solid foundation in core data skills remains essential, even as advanced tools automate parts of the machine learning pipeline. Key competencies in data wrangling, statistics, basic machine learning, and programming are prerequisites for mastering new technologies.

Essential Core Skills to Develop

- **Programming Proficiency**: Master programming languages like Python and SQL, which remain fundamental in data science and are widely supported in emerging technologies like AutoML and generative AI.
- **Statistical Knowledge**: Strong statistical knowledge helps in understanding model outputs, evaluating results, and detecting biases—a skill set that becomes even more valuable with sophisticated models.

- **Data Cleaning and Preparation**: Effective data wrangling and preparation skills ensure clean, high-quality data, which is critical to the success of advanced AI models.
- **Machine Learning Fundamentals**: Understanding foundational machine learning concepts allows data professionals to make informed decisions when using automated tools and interpreting complex models.

Preparation Tips: Regularly refresh and build on these core skills through online courses, certifications, and hands-on projects, ensuring a solid foundation to tackle more advanced topics as they emerge.

2. Learn the Basics of Emerging Technologies

While specialization can be beneficial, having a foundational understanding of emerging technologies like AutoML, reinforcement learning, and generative AI is key to staying adaptable and open to new opportunities.

Foundational Knowledge Areas for Emerging Technologies

- **AutoML**: Familiarize yourself with popular AutoML platforms like Google AutoML, H2O.ai, and DataRobot. Understand what these platforms can (and cannot) automate to effectively leverage them in projects.
- **Reinforcement Learning**: Learn the basics of reinforcement learning through courses or tutorials, exploring core concepts like agents, rewards, and policies. Experiment with simple RL environments using libraries like OpenAI Gym.

- **Generative AI**: Develop an understanding of transformer models (like GPT and BERT) and GANs (generative adversarial networks), as these models are foundational to generative AI applications. Tools like Hugging Face and TensorFlow can help you explore these models.
- **Edge and Federated Learning**: Familiarize yourself with decentralized processing and federated learning through introductory resources, focusing on applications where privacy and real-time analytics are priorities.

Preparation Tips: Take introductory courses on each of these topics to gain foundational knowledge, then experiment with simple projects using platforms and libraries. Staying updated with basic knowledge will help you pivot when more in-depth expertise is needed.

3. Experiment with New Tools and Platforms

Hands-on experience with the latest tools and platforms is essential for mastering new technologies. Experimenting with these tools allows you to understand their practical applications, limitations, and potential impact.

Popular Tools for Experimentation

- **AutoML Platforms**: Try platforms like Google Cloud AutoML, Amazon SageMaker Autopilot, or H2O.ai to automate data preprocessing, model selection, and tuning.
- **Reinforcement Learning Libraries**: Experiment with RL libraries like OpenAI Gym, Stable Baselines, or

TensorFlow-Agents to develop simple models and explore reinforcement learning.

- **Generative AI Frameworks**: Use libraries like Hugging Face Transformers for text-based generative AI or TensorFlow/Keras for implementing GANs, enabling you to create models for text, images, or audio.
- **Edge AI Development Kits**: For those interested in edge computing, explore edge AI hardware like NVIDIA Jetson or Google Coral, and software tools like TensorFlow Lite, which allow you to experiment with on-device AI.

Preparation Tips: Choose a specific tool or platform each month to explore, working on small projects that demonstrate core functionalities. This approach builds practical experience and confidence in using cutting-edge tools.

4. Engage in Continuous Learning and Stay Informed

With the rapid pace of change in AI and data science, continuous learning is a necessity. Following industry thought leaders, participating in online communities, and staying updated on research developments helps professionals remain competitive.

Methods for Continuous Learning

- **Online Courses and Certifications**: Platforms like Coursera, edX, and DataCamp offer specialized courses on emerging topics. Certifications in areas like machine learning, reinforcement learning, and data privacy can add value to your skillset.

- **Industry Conferences and Webinars**: Attend conferences like NeurIPS, ICML, and KDD, which provide insights into the latest research and developments. Online webinars and workshops from these events are also valuable for keeping up to date.
- **Follow Thought Leaders and Blogs**: Follow AI and data science thought leaders on LinkedIn, Twitter, or Medium. Blogs like Towards Data Science, Fast.ai, and OpenAI's blog provide accessible content on cutting-edge advancements.
- **Academic Journals and Research Papers**: For deeper insights, explore journals like the Journal of Machine Learning Research (JMLR) or the arXiv preprint repository. Reading research papers helps you understand upcoming trends and potential applications.

Preparation Tips: Set aside time each week for continuous learning, whether through articles, papers, or online courses. Aim to complete at least one new course or certification each quarter to stay ahead.

5. Develop Strong Data Ethics and Governance Knowledge

As machine learning technologies grow in complexity, understanding the ethical implications and governance requirements is critical. Data professionals should be prepared to address issues like data privacy, fairness, and transparency in their work.

Core Ethical and Governance Skills

- **Understanding Data Privacy Regulations**: Familiarize yourself with regulations such as GDPR and CCPA to ensure compliant data handling practices. This is particularly relevant for fields like federated learning, where data privacy is paramount.

- **Bias Detection and Fairness**: Learn to identify and mitigate biases in machine learning models. Tools like SHAP, LIME, and Fairness Indicators by Google can help assess model fairness and interpretability.
- **Transparency and Explainability**: Become proficient in using explainability tools, especially for complex models like deep learning and reinforcement learning, to build trust with stakeholders.
- **Data Security Best Practices**: Knowledge of data encryption, access controls, and decentralized processing techniques is essential for safeguarding data in cloud and edge environments.

Preparation Tips: Take online courses on data ethics, privacy, and AI fairness. Regularly review case studies to understand real-world applications and develop frameworks for ethically implementing new technologies.

6. Develop Soft Skills for Enhanced Communication and Collaboration

As data analytics becomes increasingly embedded across organizations, professionals are expected to work closely with cross-functional teams and communicate complex insights effectively. Soft skills are crucial for bridging the gap between technical findings and business objectives.

Key Soft Skills for Success

- **Effective Communication**: Simplify technical findings and present them in a way that resonates with non-technical audiences. Practice explaining complex concepts without jargon, focusing on implications and actionable insights.
- **Storytelling with Data**: Develop storytelling skills to present data in a compelling narrative format. Use tools like PowerPoint or Tableau to build engaging presentations that guide stakeholders through insights.
- **Collaboration and Teamwork**: Data projects increasingly involve collaboration with other departments, such as marketing, finance, and operations. Build rapport and foster productive working relationships to drive data-driven initiatives.
- **Critical Thinking and Problem-Solving**: As automation handles more repetitive tasks, data professionals must focus on identifying complex problems, asking the right questions, and developing creative solutions.

Preparation Tips: Join public speaking or data storytelling workshops, volunteer to present data findings within your team, and seek feedback to improve. Regular practice in communicating data insights helps build confidence and makes data professionals more effective in collaborative environments.

7. Take on Real-World Projects and Internships

Nothing accelerates learning like practical, hands-on experience. Real-world projects expose data professionals to the challenges of deploying analytics in business environments, allowing them to apply theoretical knowledge and gain a deeper understanding of advanced technologies.

Finding Real-World Learning Opportunities

- **Freelance or Consulting Projects**: Look for freelance projects or short-term consulting opportunities to apply data analytics in diverse industries, gaining exposure to practical business problems.
- **Participate in Kaggle Competitions**: Kaggle competitions offer real-world datasets and complex challenges, giving professionals a way to experiment with new techniques and learn from peers.
- **Internships and Part-Time Roles**: If possible, take internships or part-time roles that focus on areas like machine learning, data engineering, or AI, providing experience in real-world applications of analytics.
- **Collaborate with Open-Source Projects**: Contribute to open-source AI projects on platforms like GitHub to gain hands-on experience in building and deploying models in collaborative settings.

Preparation Tips: Regularly apply for small projects or collaborations and document your work in a portfolio. The hands-on experience gained from real-world projects is invaluable for building confidence and demonstrating practical expertise.

8. Create a Personal Learning Plan for Continued Growth

With so many emerging technologies and skills to master, creating a structured learning plan helps data professionals stay organized and focused. A personal learning plan can set milestones, track progress, and ensure steady development in targeted areas.

Steps to Create a Learning Plan

- **Identify Key Areas of Interest**: Based on career goals, identify areas of specialization, such as AutoML, edge AI, or generative AI, and set long-term learning goals.
- **Set Measurable Goals and Milestones**: Define specific, measurable objectives for each skill area, such as "Complete an AutoML course by Q1" or "Build a reinforcement learning model by Q2."
- **Allocate Time for Learning and Experimentation**: Dedicate regular time slots for learning, whether it's weekly online courses, monthly experiments, or quarterly certifications.
- **Review and Adjust Regularly**: Periodically assess your progress, update your plan to include new technologies, and adjust timelines as needed to ensure steady growth.

Preparation Tips: Break down learning objectives into manageable steps and celebrate small milestones to stay motivated. A learning plan keeps you focused and ensures continuous development in line with evolving trends.

Conclusion

Staying relevant and leveraging new technologies in data analytics requires a proactive approach to learning, experimentation, and skill development. By building a solid foundation, exploring emerging technologies, developing soft skills, and embracing hands-on projects, data professionals can position themselves at the forefront of an evolving field. A commitment to continuous learning, coupled with a structured personal learning plan, ensures that data professionals are well-prepared to harness new technologies, create meaningful impact, and remain competitive in a fast-paced, technology-driven world.

References for "Future of Data Analytics and Machine Learning"

1. **Aggarwal, C. C. (2018)**. *Machine Learning for Text*. Springer.
   - An in-depth resource covering machine learning techniques in text processing, including applications in natural language processing (NLP).
2. **Alpaydin, E. (2020)**. *Introduction to Machine Learning (4th ed.)*. MIT Press.
   - This book provides a comprehensive introduction to machine learning, from fundamental concepts to more advanced topics.
3. **Barredo Arrieta, A., et al. (2020)**. "Explainable Artificial Intelligence (XAI): Concepts, Taxonomies, Opportunities and Challenges toward Responsible AI." *Information Fusion*, 58, 82-115.
   - An article providing a detailed overview of explainable AI, addressing techniques for making machine learning models interpretable and transparent.
4. **Bengio, Y., Goodfellow, I., & Courville, A. (2016)**. *Deep Learning*. MIT Press.
   - A foundational book on deep learning, covering neural networks, generative adversarial networks (GANs), and applications in various fields.

242

5. **Brownlee, J. (2021)**. *Automated Machine Learning (AutoML): The Next Wave of Machine Learning*. Machine Learning Mastery.
    o A guide on AutoML, discussing how automation is transforming the machine learning pipeline and making data science more accessible.
6. **Chollet, F. (2021)**. *Deep Learning with Python (2nd ed.)*. Manning Publications.
    o An introduction to deep learning with practical examples in Python, including applications of generative AI and reinforcement learning.
7. **Das, A., & McAfee, R. (2021)**. *Machine Learning for Decision Makers: Cognitive Computing Fundamentals for Better Decision Making*. Packt Publishing.
    o This book bridges technical machine learning with strategic business insights, ideal for understanding the impact of AI on decision-making.
8. **Géron, A. (2019)**. *Hands-On Machine Learning with Scikit-Learn, Keras, and TensorFlow (2nd ed.)*. O'Reilly Media.
    o A hands-on guide covering a wide array of machine learning and deep learning techniques, with practical examples in Python.
9. **Goodfellow, I., Pouget-Abadie, J., Mirza, M., et al. (2014)**. "Generative Adversarial Networks." *arXiv preprint arXiv:1406.2661.*

- The foundational paper introducing GANs, explaining the competitive training between the generator and discriminator models.

10. **Hastie, T., Tibshirani, R., & Friedman, J. (2009).** *The Elements of Statistical Learning: Data Mining, Inference, and Prediction (2nd ed.).* Springer.
    - A comprehensive guide on statistical learning and machine learning, suitable for data science and analytics professionals.

11. **Howard, J., & Gugger, S. (2020).** *Deep Learning for Coders with Fastai and PyTorch.* O'Reilly Media.
    - A practical resource for building and deploying deep learning models, focusing on PyTorch and Fastai for real-world applications.

12. **Koller, D., & Friedman, N. (2009).** *Probabilistic Graphical Models: Principles and Techniques.* MIT Press.
    - This book introduces graphical models, which are key in reinforcement learning and probabilistic approaches to machine learning.

13. **Li, J., & Chen, S. (2021).** *AutoML: Concepts and Applications.* Springer.
    - An overview of automated machine learning, discussing its applications, benefits, and challenges in simplifying the machine learning pipeline.

14. **Ng, A. (2020).** *Machine Learning Yearning.* DeepLearning.AI.

- A guide focused on practical tips and strategies for building successful machine learning projects, including advice on data preparation and model iteration.

15. **O'Reilly, C. (2019)**. *Data Governance: Creating an Environment of Data Quality and Integrity*. Elsevier.
    - This book covers essential topics in data governance, including compliance, security, and the role of governance in AI and machine learning projects.

16. **OpenAI (2021)**. "Language Models are Few-Shot Learners." *arXiv preprint arXiv:2005.14165*.
    - The paper introducing GPT-3, explaining the transformer model architecture and its applications in generative AI.

17. **Raschka, S., & Mirjalili, V. (2019)**. *Python Machine Learning (3rd ed.)*. Packt Publishing.
    - An accessible book covering practical machine learning applications in Python, from basic machine learning to advanced deep learning topics.

18. **Russell, S. J., & Norvig, P. (2020)**. *Artificial Intelligence: A Modern Approach (4th ed.)*. Pearson.
    - A widely used textbook on AI, covering a broad range of topics including reinforcement learning, probabilistic reasoning, and ethical considerations.

19. **Sharma, H. (2022)**. *Explainable AI with Python: Understand Data-Driven Decisions through Explainability*. Packt Publishing.

   o A guide to implementing explainable AI techniques, with Python examples that make complex models interpretable and trustworthy.

20. **Silver, D., Sutton, R., & Barto, A. (2018)**. *Reinforcement Learning: An Introduction (2nd ed.)*. MIT Press.

   o The primary textbook on reinforcement learning, introducing key concepts like Q-learning, policy gradients, and applications in dynamic environments.

21. **Vallabhaneni, V., & Srinivasa, N. (2021)**. *Edge AI: Convergence of Edge Computing and Artificial Intelligence*. Springer.

   o An exploration of edge AI, discussing how AI at the edge of networks is used in real-time analytics, IoT, and privacy-sensitive applications.

22. **Vapnik, V. (1998)**. *Statistical Learning Theory*. Wiley-Interscience.

   o A foundational text on statistical learning, offering insights into the theory behind machine learning models, including support vector machines.

23. **Zhou, Z. (2021)**. *Federated Learning: Collaborative Machine Learning without Centralized Training Data*. Springer.

- An introduction to federated learning, explaining how decentralized models are trained to preserve privacy in data-sensitive applications.
24. **Zhou, Z.-H. (2022)**. *Machine Learning (2nd ed.)*. Springer.
    - An advanced yet accessible book on machine learning, covering both foundational concepts and modern applications like generative models and federated learning.

Online Resources and Communities

- **arXiv.org** – A repository of research papers in AI and machine learning, where professionals can stay updated on cutting-edge research.
- **Kaggle** – A platform offering datasets and competitions, providing hands-on practice with real-world data science problems.
- **Towards Data Science on Medium** – A blog covering tutorials, industry trends, and discussions on machine learning, data analytics, and AI.
- **Data Science Central** – An online resource offering articles, webinars, and community discussions on trends and tools in data science.
- **Coursera and edX** – Platforms offering online courses from top universities on machine learning, AutoML, reinforcement learning, and data ethics.

These resources provide a foundational understanding of data analytics and machine learning, essential for data professionals adapting to emerging trends and technologies.

About the Author

Dr, Alex Harper

Driven by a passion for data-driven insights and their transformative impact on business and technology, Dr. Alex Harper has dedicated their career to advancing data analytics and empowering professionals through accessible, practical knowledge. Building upon the foundations laid in their previous books, *Essential Data Analytics: Quick-Start Guide to Data Literacy for Beginners* and *Intermediate Data Analytic Skills: Databases, Programming, and Advanced Statistics*, they continue to explore complex data concepts with a clear, approachable style.

With over a decade of experience in the field, Dr. Alex Harper combines deep technical knowledge with a commitment to ethical data practices and a strong focus on real-world applications. Their expertise spans statistical analysis, machine learning, and advanced analytics, equipping readers with the skills necessary to thrive in an evolving data landscape. In this ongoing series, they expand into advanced topics, offering comprehensive guidance on machine learning, data mining, and analytic thinking to help readers at every stage of their data journey.

Beyond authoring, Dr. Alex Harper is a sought-after speaker and advisor in data literacy and analytics education, frequently collaborating with industry experts to bridge the gap between complex analytics concepts and their practical use. This dedication has earned them recognition as a leading voice in data analytics, inspiring a new generation of data-driven thinkers.

Disclaimer

This book is intended for informational and educational purposes only. The author and publisher have made every effort to ensure the accuracy and completeness of the information contained within; however, they assume no responsibility for errors, omissions, or changes to the data and methodologies discussed. The content of this book should not be interpreted as professional advice, and readers are encouraged to seek expert consultation for specific issues related to data analytics, machine learning, or any other technical topics covered herein.

The use of any tools, techniques, or recommendations provided in this book is at the reader's discretion and risk. The author and publisher are not liable for any damages, losses, or claims resulting from the application of information in this book, nor do they endorse any third-party products or services mentioned. All trademarks, product names, and company names mentioned in this book are the property of their respective owners and are used solely for identification purposes.

The reader is encouraged to verify current laws, regulations, and industry standards, as these may impact the application of data analytics techniques discussed in this book. This book is not a substitute for legal, regulatory, or technical expertise in the fields discussed.

Legal Notice

This book is provided "as is" without warranty of any kind, either express or implied, including but not limited to the implied warranties of merchantability, fitness for a particular purpose, or non-infringement. The author and publisher disclaim any liability, loss, or risk incurred as a consequence, directly or indirectly, of the use and application of any of the contents of this book.

The information contained in this book is intended for general informational purposes only and does not constitute professional, legal, or financial advice. The strategies and techniques discussed may not be suitable for every individual or situation, and readers should consult with a qualified professional before applying the information to their specific circumstances. The author and publisher make no representations or warranties with respect to the accuracy or completeness of the contents of this book and specifically disclaim any liability for any damages, losses, or risks, whether direct, indirect, incidental, or consequential, incurred as a result of the use or application of any of the information provided herein.

All trademarks, service marks, product names, or named features are the property of their respective owners, and no claim is made by the author or publisher to any such mark or other intellectual property. The inclusion of any organization, website, or product name does not imply endorsement or affiliation.

By reading this book, you agree to assume all risks associated with the use of the information provided and release the author and publisher from any and all claims, liabilities, or damages that may arise from such use.